D1595189

Southern Seasons

Southern Seasons

CONTEMPORARY REGIONAL CUISINE

Happy Cooking!
Come back
— JARED

Robert St. John   Wyatt Waters

DIFFERENT DRUMMER PRESS   HATTIESBURG

Copyright © Different Drummer Press

Artworks © Wyatt Waters

All right reserved

Manufactured in Canada

Trade Edition: ISBN 10: 0-9721972-3-0, ISBN 13: 978-0-9721972-3-6

University of Mississippi Limited Edition: ISBN 10: 0-9721972-4-9, ISBN 13: 978-0-9721972-4-3

Mississippi State University Limited Edition: ISBN 10: 0-9721972-5-7, ISBN 13: 978-0-9721972-5-0

University of Southern Mississippi Limited Edition: ISBN 10: 0-9721972-6-5, ISBN 13: 978-0-9721972-6-7

Mississippi Development Authority Limited Edition: ISBN 10: 0-9721972-7-3, ISBN 13: 978-0-9721972-7-4

Visit www.robertstjohn.com

or visit Robert's restaurants:

The Purple Parrot Café, The Crescent City Grill, and The Mahogany Bar

3904 Hardy Street Hattiesburg, MS 39402, 601-264-0656

519 Azalea Drive Meridian, MS 39301, 601-553-3656

www.nsrg.com

Visit the Wyatt Waters Gallery

307 Jefferson Street

Clinton, MS 39056

Phone - (601)925-8115

www.wyattwaters.com

Design and production by John A. Langston

Photographs on page 2 by Michael Goldsholl

The following artworks are reproduced with the generous cooperation of the owners:

Boo Radleys—collection of Ann Copland

Indian Summer—collection of Butler, Snow, O'Mara, Stevens, and Cannada, PLLC

Naked Ladies—collection of Alice and Graham Smith

Old Maids—collection of Jennifer and Aaron Boucher

On Top of Old Smoky—collection of Fred and Jean Adams

White Bloomers—collection of Larry and Cindy Stuart

Yes M'am, Gnome—collection of Tara Lytal

Walking in Memphis and *To Everything Churn, Churn, Churn*—
    collection of Kay Cooper Gabbert and Craig Gabbert

To strong-willed Southern Ladies:
Jill, Vicki, Holleman, Crimson, Dinny, and Lucy

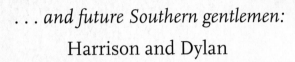

. . . and future Southern gentlemen:
Harrison and Dylan

In Memory of Jennifer Johnson Pender

Contents

Introduction

In the spring of 2001, a regular customer of the Purple Parrot Café introduced me to a publisher.

She had been hounding me for years, "Robert, why don't you write a cookbook?" I had given her excuse after excuse as to why I was too busy to spend time writing a book, but she persisted.

The customer called me over to her table and introduced me to the publisher. His first question was, "Robert, if you were going to write a cookbook, what would it look like?"

I didn't have a cookbook in mind, nor had I given any thought to ever publishing a cookbook. Trying to think quickly, I said, "If I were to do a cookbook, I would have recipes that I have developed at the restaurant over the years. I would include a few of my favorite essays that have been published in my newspaper column, and I would have watercolors by Wyatt Waters."

Without missing a beat, the publisher said, "If you can get Wyatt Waters, you've got a deal." It was as easy as that; one man's name had just inked a book deal.

There was one seemingly large problem— I didn't know Wyatt Waters.

Resolved at this point that I was going to write a book, I hopped in my car and drove to the Wyatt Waters Gallery in Clinton, Mississippi. I introduced myself, told the artist of my conversation with the publisher, and shared with him my thoughts on a collaborative book project.

We hit it off immediately, a friendship was formed, a professional partnership began, and the work that was to be our first collaboration was born.

After having a difference of opinion with the "book experts" on the design of the book (they wanted a black-and-white spiral-bound version), we parted ways with the publisher and I formed a publishing company with the intent to design and release a coffee-table cookbook with the working title *A Southern Palate.*

The process was simple: Wyatt asked that I give him copies of the recipes and stories I planned to use and, over the course of the next year, he painted the 32 watercolors that would become the visual core of the book. It was the defining element and one that took a simple collection of recipes, representing a 14-year restaurant career, and a few humorous stories into a new category of publication. To my knowledge, it had never been done before.

A steady schedule of book signings and cooking demos were scheduled for the book's release, and all was well until the West Coast dock strike of 2002. The books, which had been printed in Hong Kong, were being held captive on a dock somewhere near Long Beach, California, another victim of the never-ending struggle of labor vs. management.

The daily stress level was high. The Christmas season was key to the book's success and it was approaching rapidly. I had depleted my meager savings and investment accounts to pay for the costs of publishing and printing the book. Bookstores, museums, and Junior Leaguers were waiting for the release. We were, too.

No one had any idea as to when the strike would be resolved. For three weeks the news changed hourly. One minute it looked as if the strike would be settled and the books would be loaded onto a truck that day. The next report we received would tell of the books hopefully arriving sometime in January.

Ultimately the strike was resolved two days before the first scheduled book signing. A truck driver drove day and night, miles beyond the governmentally allotted mileage, to reach his destination. A truckload of 10,000 books arrived at my restaurant office in Hattiesburg, Mississippi at 10 a.m. on October 30, 2002. The first book signing was scheduled for 5 p.m. that afternoon. Three weeks later the books were gone.

Looking back, it was one of the most exciting periods of my life. Actually, shy of my children being born and my wedding day, it was the most exciting time of my life.

There were lines everywhere we went. At Mistletoe Marketplace, a three-day holiday shopping event in Jackson, Mississippi, we signed 3,000 books in three days. There was a continual long line in front of our table in the Mississippi Trade Mart from 9 a.m. until 9 p.m. Some of those waiting in line had heard of the book, others just saw a line, took their place in it, and when they reached our table said, "I don't know what you are selling, but I saw the line, and I got in it hoping not to miss out on whatever it was that those people were waiting for." It was nuts.

Since the first book signing was scheduled seven hours after the books arrived we didn't have the luxury of shipping cases of books via common carrier. Wyatt and I served as deliverymen during the three-week period, personally loading and unloading a majority of the 10,000 books.

The frenzy began instantly. We traveled the state from top to bottom in a beat-up SUV with bald tires. Everyone wanted books. After the initial deliveries, there were none to be had.

We rushed to have a second printing completed before Christmas and were told the books wouldn't arrive until January. Working from the hip, we quickly threw together a gift package that included a certificate for the book and a limited edition print by Wyatt which sold out in two weeks. The craziness had grown from people trying to purchase a book, to people purchasing the promise of a book.

A three-week sell-out of a small, self-published book sold from a tiny restaurant office in Hattiesburg with no marketing strategy or budget was unheard of. I had no idea. This was my first time out of the chute. We signed books until we lost all of the feeling in our right index fingers and thumbs, and then we signed some more.

Everyone seemed to love the book. The art was a hit, the recipes were sampled and eaten, and the "My South" essay— making its first published appearance outside of a newspaper column or forwarded email— continued to generate buzz.

We held the first of what would turn out to be over 100 dual-demos in which Wyatt painted a still life, and I cooked a four-course seafood summer supper using recipes from the book, all in a matter of 90 minutes.

Some demos were performed under battlefield conditions. Early on, in a department store in Jackson somewhere near the cosmetics counter, we blew circuits and lost electricity and had no heat with which to cook. At the same time, Wyatt was trying to finish a watercolor painting without the aid of water.

In another department store in either Chattanooga or Knoxville, we almost caught a rack of panties on fire while performing our dual-demo in the lingerie section. We learned quickly that the switch from electricity to propane had its challenges. Nevertheless, Wyatt had water to work with and we moved up the personal appearance ladder from department stores to cooking-demo showplaces such as The Everyday Gourmet in Jackson and Viking Culinary Arts Centers throughout the country.

After the craziness died down and the feeling returned to our fingers and digits, we talked about a follow-up project.

The temptation to follow-up our success immediately riding the wave of momentum from the first book was tempting. I was energized and ready to go. Wyatt— the one with the cooler head and more even temperament— felt that the timing wasn't right. He was correct.

In the following years, Wyatt published another book and illustrated several more. I released two more books and then I signed book deals with two publishers releasing two more cookbooks and a work of non-fiction. All the while Wyatt and I were working on the book that you currently hold in your hands.

Southern Seasons has been a five-year labor of love.

We wanted to focus on seasons in the South (to the extent that there are seasons in the South). Some say the South's seasonal calendar doesn't consist of spring, summer, fall, and winter, but: almost summer, summer, still summer, and Christmas. Others track the seasons as: dove, deer, duck, and turkey. Still others measure the seasons of the year as: football season, basketball season, and baseball season. In my part of the state we have been guilty of focusing on crab season, crawfish season, shrimp season, and oyster season.

This book focuses on seasons of color, seasons of taste, and seasons of life. Wyatt says, "It's the kind of book you can start in the middle and go to the end. It's a cycle. It puts you in touch with the seasons."

This time around I reversed the creative process. Instead of giving Wyatt my recipes first, I asked for his artwork. I used the beautiful paintings published herein as inspiration to create seasonal menus and recipes.

Whether this book is as successful as *A Southern Palate* remains to be seen. It has almost twice the artwork and the recipes were developed specifically for this project. Out of the five cookbooks I have written since that first effort, I believe that this collection of recipes is the finest I have developed.

Ultimately, this book is about our vision and impressions of the South, its people, its culture, and its food. And regardless of book sales, book signings, and notoriety, I have been fortunate to have made a lifelong friend.

The friends one makes early in childhood seem to be the longest and deepest relationships. I can go five years without seeing a buddy from junior high school, and we reacquaint instantly as if we haven't missed a day. It is rare that one makes such a friend later in life.

I have made a true friend in Wyatt Waters. If nothing else came from the publishing process, striking up a lifelong friendship would be more than enough and well worth the effort.

As hectic as the early days of *A Southern Palate* were, they are the fondest memories of a 25-year professional career. Through union strikes, power outages, department store droughts, flaming panties, numb fingers, bald tires and all— as with most of the good things that have happened in my life— this new journey was unplanned but much enjoyed.

Robert St. John

Acknowledgments

First and foremost thanks to my friend, co-writer, collaborator, co-conspirator, and fellow Beatle fanatic, Wyatt Waters. The most humble, generous, and talented man I know.

A world of thanks to Linda Nance, Chef de Cuisine, Purple Parrot Café—for recipe testing, long hours, hard days, and culinary counsel

The Purple Parrot recipe-testing crew—Jeremy Noffke, Scott Strickland, Rebecca Whittington, Monique Hoard, Neville Barr, and Colby Stark

John Langston—book producer and designer for getting it done under the wire

Anne Stascavage—copy editor and red-ink warrior who possibly had the toughest job of all

Stacey Andrews and Maria Keyes—who handle the day-in-day-out craziness in the three-ring circus

Clint Taylor, New South Restaurant Group, Managing Partner—for continuing to hold down the fort, and doing a mighty fine job of it

Michael Goldsholl, photographer for making the best of a challenging situation

Fred Carl, Carol Puckett, and Jane Crump of Mississippi's Viking Range Corporation, for years of support

Customers of the Purple Parrot Café, Crescent City Grill, and Mahogany Bar who continue to make it all possible

Readers of my weekly column who sometimes know more about me than I care to remember

The independent bookstores on the front lines of the book business, especially Main Street Books in my hometown of Hattiesburg, MS, Lemuria Books in Jackson, MS, and Square Books in Oxford, MS

Shane and Ronnie who keep me propped up as I try to straddle the straight-and-narrow

Jill, Holleman, and Harrison—My rock and my reason

New Year's Day

Barbara Jane's Layered Cream Cheese Spread

Hoppin' John

Hoisin Glazed Chicken Wings

Sesame-Soy Cabbage Stir-Fry

Sautéed Garlic Shrimp

Smoked Tuna Pasta Salad

Creamy Balsamic Vinaigrette Dressing

Yes M'am, Gnome
If this gnome could talk he might get someone in trouble. New Year's Eve is followed by New Year's Day, a recovery period from an intense holiday marathon intermingled with football games, eating, and resolutions to lose weight.

Barbara Jane's
Layered Cream Cheese Spread

Barbara Jane Foote is one of my favorite home cooks. She served a variation of this dish to my wife and me on a visit to her home. I bugged her for two months for the recipe. It is tweaked a little from her preparation but the original spirit and intent are there.

2 tablespoons olive oil

¼ cup onion, minced

1 teaspoon garlic, minced

1½ teaspoons Creole Seasoning (recipe page 21)

1 10-ounce package frozen spinach, thawed and squeezed dry

1 pound sharp cheddar cheese, grated

⅓ cup mayonnaise

3 tablespoons sour cream

½ cup toasted pecans, chopped

1 tablespoon Creole mustard

1 tablespoon fresh parsley, chopped

2 8-ounce packages cream cheese, softened

¼ teaspoon salt

½ teaspoon black pepper, freshly ground

⅛ teaspoon cayenne pepper

½ cup peach or apricot preserves

¼ cup green onions, minced

¼ teaspoon ground nutmeg

Line a 9 x 5-inch loaf pan with plastic wrap.

Heat olive oil in a medium sauté pan over medium heat. Cook onions 3–4 minutes. Stir in garlic and Creole Seasoning, cooking 2 more minutes. Stir in spinach and blend well. Remove mixture from heat and allow to cool.

In a mixing bowl, stir together the cheddar cheese, mayonnaise, sour cream, toasted pecans, Creole mustard, and parsley. Blend well and spread half of the mixture into the bottom of the lined loaf pan.

In a separate bowl, combine 1 package of the cream cheese and the cooled spinach mixture. Blend well and spread over the first cheddar-pecan layer of the loaf. Spread the remaining cheddar mixture over the spinach mixture.

Tin Below

The South has its share of twisters and when weather gets tough, the tough get going to the storm shelter. Just the thought of the tornado from the *Wizard of Oz* sends a chill.

Using the paddle attachment of an electric mixer, beat remaining cream cheese until light and creamy. Add salt, black pepper, cayenne pepper, preserves, green onions, and nutmeg. Spread final layer on top of the loaf and wrap very tightly with plastic wrap. Refrigerate for 4–6 hours before serving (also freezes well, but must thaw 8 hours before serving).

To serve, sink the loaf pan into a warm water bath for 1–2 minutes. Do not let water seep into plastic and reach mold. Unmold onto serving platter and remove plastic wrap.

Yield: 20–25 appetizer servings

Hoppin' John

The quintessential New Year's Day dish in the South.

1 cup spicy sausage, small dice
1 cup smoked sausage, small dice
1 cup onion, diced
½ cup celery, diced
½ cup bell pepper, diced
1 tablespoon garlic, minced
1 teaspoon salt
½ teaspoon pepper
1 teaspoon Creole Seasoning (recipe follows)
½ cup rice
2 cups chicken broth, hot
1 recipe Black-Eyed Peas (recipe follows)
1 tablespoon hot sauce

Preheat oven to 325°.

Place the diced meats in a medium saucepan over low-medium heat. Cook 6–7 minutes, stirring often to prevent sticking. Add onion, celery, pepper, and garlic and continue to cook 10 minutes. Add salt, pepper, Creole Seasoning, and rice and cook long enough to allow the rice to get hot. Add the chicken broth and bring to a simmer. Lower heat and cover the saucepan. Cook 15 minutes (there should still be some broth in the pot).

While the mixture is simmering, puree 1 cup of the cooked black-eyed peas. Add the whole peas, the pureed peas, and hot sauce to the rice mixture. Mix well and pour into a 2-quart baking dish. Cover with foil and place in oven for 30–45 minutes. Remove foil and bake an additional 20–30 minutes. Remove and serve.

Yield: 8–10 servings

BLACK-EYED PEAS

3 cups fresh black-eyed peas
4 cups Pork Stock (recipe follows)
1 piece bacon
2 teaspoons sugar
2 teaspoons salt
1 tablespoon flour

Place peas, stock, bacon, sugar, and salt in a 2-quart saucepan over medium heat. Bring to a boil. Reduce heat to a slow simmer and cover. Simmer 30–45 minutes. Remove ¼ cup of potliquor. Stir flour into potliquor and pour back into peas. Bring back to a simmer and cook 10 minutes more. Remove from heat and let rest for 10 minutes before serving.

Yield: 6–8 servings

PORK STOCK

8 ham hocks
1½ gallons water
½ onion

Place hocks, water, and onion in a large stockpot and simmer over low heat 8 hours. Add more water as needed to yield 1 gallon of final product. Strain and place stock in refrigerator overnight. Using a large spoon, remove fat layer from top of chilled stock. Stock should be slightly gelatinous. Stock can be frozen in small batches.

Yield: 1 gallon

Note: Reserve ham hock meat for other recipes

CREOLE SEASONING

½ cup Lawry's Seasoned Salt
2 tablespoon onion powder
2 tablespoon paprika
1 Tablespoon cayenne pepper
1 Tablespoon white pepper
1 tablespoon + 1 teaspoon garlic powder
1 Tablespooon black pepper
1 teaspoon dry mustard
1 teaspoon oregano, dry
1 teaspoon thyme, dry

Combine all ingredients.

Hoisin Glazed Chicken Wings

Hoisin is one of my favorite oriental sauces. Don't wait until New Year's Day to make these. Make plenty and make them often.

1 gallon + ¼ cup water
⅓ cup soy sauce
⅓ cup sugar
2 tablespoons kosher salt
1½ tablespoons crushed red pepper flakes
½ cup white vinegar
2 tablespoons fresh ginger, minced
3 pounds fresh chicken wings
2 7-ounce jars hoisin sauce
¼ cup sugar
1 tablespoon fresh jalapeños, small dice
2 teaspoons garlic, minced
1 tablespoon fresh lime juice
1 tablespoon hot sauce

In a large stock pot, combine the gallon of water, soy sauce, sugar, salt, red pepper flakes, vinegar, and ginger. Bring mixture to a simmer, and cook 10 minutes.

Place the chicken wings in the simmering mixture. Once the water returns to a simmer, cook the wings 20 minutes.

Using a large colander, strain chicken and discard the liquid. Let wings cool in the refrigerator 1 hour. This step can be done 1–2 days in advance.

Preheat oven to 250°. Line a large baking sheet with heavy-duty aluminum foil and set aside.

In a mixing bowl, stir together the hoisin sauce, sugar, ¼ cup water, jalapeños, garlic, lime juice, and hot sauce. Remove half of this mixture for later use.

Toss the precooked wings in the mixing bowl, coating them well with the sauce. Arrange on the foil-lined baking sheet and cover them completely with another sheet of aluminum foil. Bake 50 minutes.

Remove foil and place the remaining sauce in a large mixing bowl. Gently place the wings in the bowl, and toss with the sauce. Return the wings to the baking sheet. Turn the oven up to 275° and return the wings to the oven, uncovered, for 45 minutes. Remove from the oven and serve.

Yield: 8–10 servings

Turn Right at the Big Chicken
In Marietta, Georgia, there is a fried chicken stand that caused a ruckus. Some thought it an eyesore. Others considered it art. Whatever your opinion, it's an unmistakable landmark.

Sesame-Soy Cabbage Stir-Fry

A very unique twist on a standby stir-fry dish. Don't be afraid to substitute your favorite cabbage.

¼ cup peanut oil or vegetable oil
1 tablespoon fresh ginger, minced
1 tablespoon garlic, minced
¼ teaspoon crushed red chili flakes
½ cup red onion, peeled and julienned
¾ cup carrot, julienned
¾ cup red bell pepper, julienned
1 head bok choy, leaves cut crosswise into ½-inch-thick slices (approximately 5–6 cups cut)
6 green onions, trimmed, cut diagonally into 1-inch pieces
1½ cups fresh snow peas
½ head Napa cabbage, leaves cut crosswise into 1-inch-wide strips (about 3–4 cups cut)
⅔ cup good-quality chicken stock or broth or vegetable broth
¼ cup soy sauce
1 tablespoon cornstarch, dissolved in 1 tablespoon cold water
2 tablespoons toasted sesame seeds

Heat a large wok over medium heat. Add 2 tablespoons of the oil. When the oil is hot, add the ginger, garlic, and chili flakes and stir-fry just until aromatic, approximately 30 seconds. Scoop out the aromatics and set them aside.

Add the remaining oil to the wok. Turn heat to high. When the oil is hot, add onion, carrot, and red pepper and cook until glossy and bright, 1–2 minutes.

Add the bok choy. Stir-fry 1–2 minutes more. Add green onions and snow peas. Continue stir-frying until they are bright green and glossy, 1–2 minutes more. Add the Napa cabbage along with about ⅓ cup of the hot stock and the reserved aromatics. Continue stir-frying until the vegetables are all tender-crisp, about 2 minutes more. Add the remaining stock, soy sauce, and cornstarch mixture and stir-fry until the vegetables appear lightly glazed with sauce, approximately 1 minute more.

Transfer the stir-fried vegetables to a heated serving dish. Garnish with toasted sesame seeds and serve immediately.

Yield: 8–10 servings

Sautéed Garlic Shrimp

We serve this dish in the Crescent City Grill. It should always be served with plenty of French bread for dipping and sopping. There is so much flavor in the sauce, each piece of bread is almost like having an extra shrimp.

2 pounds (21–25) shrimp, peeled and deveined
1 teaspoon kosher salt
1 teaspoon Creole Seasoning (recipe page 21)
½ teaspoon black pepper, freshly ground
3 tablespoons olive oil
1½ tablespoons garlic, minced
¼ cup white wine
½ cup chicken broth
1 cup Wishbone Italian Dressing
¼ cup unsalted butter, cut into small cubes
2 tablespoons fresh parsley, chopped

Season the shrimp with the salt, Creole Seasoning, and black pepper.

Place olive oil in a large, heavy-duty sauté pan over high heat. Heat oil until it just begins to smoke. Carefully place the shrimp in the smoking hot pan. Allow shrimp to cook without moving them for 3–4 minutes. Add the garlic and stir the shrimp. Cook shrimp 3 minutes more. Add the white wine and allow it to reduce almost completely. Add chicken broth and Italian dressing and cook until the sauce begins to simmer. Cook shrimp 3 minutes in the simmering sauce. Add the butter cubes and blend into the simmering sauce.

Remove the shrimp from the heat and stir in the parsley. Serve immediately.

Yield: 8–10 servings

Smoked Tuna Pasta Salad

Tried and true. A longtime favorite of Crescent City Grill customers. It's great for summer picnics, too. Don't overcook the tuna on the smoker or it will be extremely dry.

1 pound fresh tuna (whole loin or fresh steaks)
2½ cups Creamy Balsamic Vinaigrette Dressing (recipe follows)
½ pound dry rotini pasta
1 cup black olives, sliced
1 cup red onion, peeled and small dice
½ cup red bell pepper, small dice
½ cup green bell pepper, small dice
1 cup fresh tomato, medium dice
1 teaspoon salt
1 teaspoon freshly ground black pepper
¼ cup fresh parsley, chopped

Rub the outside of the tuna thoroughly with ½ cup of the Creamy Balsamic Vinaigrette Dressing and let marinate 2–3 hours. Using your outdoor grill, smoke the tuna slowly until it reaches medium to medium-well. Refrigerate the smoked tuna.

When tuna has cooled completely, dice it into ¾-inch cubes.

Following the directions on the package of rotini, cook the pasta. Once the pasta is cooked, drain well and rinse thoroughly with cool water. Drain completely.

Place pasta in a large mixing bowl. Add all of the remaining ingredients and the tuna and mix well. Chill for 2–3 hours before serving.

Yield: 8–10 servings

Creamy Balsamic Vinaigrette Dressing

This is the house dressing I created for the Crescent City Grill.

3 egg yolks
2 eggs
½ teaspoon dry mustard
2 tablespoons garlic, minced
½ teaspoon white pepper
1 teaspoon garlic salt
⅛ teaspoon cayenne pepper
2 tablespoons fresh parsley, chopped
2 teaspoons dried oregano
2 tablespoons red wine vinegar
¼ cup balsamic vinegar
1 teaspoon salt
1 cup ranch dressing
1 cup cottonseed oil or canola oil

Combine all ingredients in the bowl of a food processor except ranch dressing and oil. Mix well. With the machine running, slowly drizzle in ranch dressing and then cottonseed oil. Refrigerate until ready to use. This dressing will hold 1 week refrigerated.

Yield: 3 cups

Mardi Gras Brunch

Fruit Salad with Sour Cream-Grenadine Dressing

Tasso and Biscuits with Blackberry Preserves

Shrimp and Okra Gumbo

Shrimp Stock

Mardi Gras Brunch Casserole

Grillades and Grits

King Cake Bread Pudding

NOLA
A little plastic Jesus was hidden inside king cakes of yore. Whoever found the king in the cake gave the next party. Choking liability has forced the king to be placed outside of today's cakes.

PAGES 28–29:
Spring, Sprang, Sprung
Just when you think Winter is going to last forever, yellow daffodils appear announcing Spring's arrival. These are the lemon-yellow petal with the orange-yellow trumpet variety.

Fruit Salad with Sour Cream–Grenadine Dressing

An early lunch stalwart in the Purple Parrot Café and still one that shows up on the feature selections throughout the summer. Don't cut the apple or banana until the lemon juice and sugar are combined. Place fruit in the lemon juice mixture as soon as it is cut.

2 tablespoons fresh lemon juice
2 tablespoons sugar
1 banana, peeled and sliced into ½-inch round pieces
1 large red delicious apple, core removed, medium dice (about 1½ cups)
1 cup red seedless grapes
1½ cups green seedless grapes
2 cups fresh pineapple, skin and core removed, medium dice
½ cup orange segments
1½ cups cantaloupe, peeled, seeded, and small dice
1 pint fresh strawberries, hull removed and berries quartered
¾ cup sour cream
2 tablespoons grenadine

In a large mixing bowl, combine the lemon juice and sugar. Toss the apples and bananas in the mixture to prevent them from turning brown. Add the remaining fruit. In a small mixing bowl, whisk together the sour cream and grenadine. Add the sour cream mixture to the fruit and stir together, coating the fruit completely. Hold covered in the refrigerator until ready to serve. Just before serving, toss the fruit once more to redistribute the dressing.

Yield: 8–10 servings

Tasso and Biscuits
with Blackberry Preserves

Good for breakfast, brunch, or a cocktail party (or for a midday or midnight snack). I love these—they taste like the South. Tasso is Cajun-spiced ham; make sure to shave it thin. Country ham or smoked ham can be substituted.

2 cups flour
1 tablespoon sugar
1½ teaspoons baking soda
1 teaspoon baking powder
1½ teaspoons kosher salt
½ teaspoon Poultry Seasoning (recipe page 111)
½ cup butter, cut into small cubes and frozen
1 egg
¾ cup buttermilk
3 tablespoons unsalted butter, melted
½ cup blackberry preserves
¼ pound tasso ham, shaved very thin

Preheat oven to 375°.

In a food processor combine flour, sugar, baking soda, baking powder, salt, and poultry seasoning; pulse to mix. Add the frozen butter, pulsing until mixture resembles coarse bread crumbs. Transfer mixture to a large mixing bowl and make a well in the center. In a small bowl, whisk together the egg and buttermilk. Pour buttermilk mixture into the well and gently blend together the dough, being careful not to overmix.

Allow the dough to set for 10 minutes and then turn dough onto a floured surface. Gently knead dough for 1–2 minutes. Roll out to ¾-inch thickness. Cut 1½-inch circles from the dough and place them on an ungreased baking sheet. Brush the tops with the melted butter.

Bake 12–15 minutes.

Cut biscuits in half lengthwise. Spread 1 teaspoon of blackberry preserves on the bottom half of the biscuit. Add 2 thinly shaved pieces of tasso and replace the top half of the biscuit. Serve warm.

Yield: 6–8 servings

Shrimp and Okra Gumbo

Make sure and get the roux as dark as possible without burning it. A dark roux is the key to good gumbo. If you burn it, throw it out. It can't be saved. I like my gumbo with extra rice.

½ cup canola oil
¾ cup flour
2 tablespoons filé powder
1 cup onion, diced
½ cup celery, diced
½ cup bell pepper, diced
1½ cups fresh okra, sliced
2 tablespoons garlic, minced
2 teaspoons salt
1½ teaspoons black pepper
2 teaspoons Creole Seasoning (recipe page 21)
1 teaspoon dried thyme
1½ pounds shrimp, small
2 quarts shrimp stock (recipe following)
1 cup tomatoes, diced, canned or fresh
1 tablespoon hot sauce
¼ teaspoon cayenne pepper
2 cups cooked white rice

In a large skillet, combine oil, flour, and filé powder to form a roux. Cook over medium heat, stirring often until roux is very dark (be careful not to burn). Add vegetables, garlic, spices, and shrimp and continue to cook for 5–7 minutes, stirring constantly to prevent burning. Meanwhile, bring shrimp stock and tomatoes to a boil. Slowly add roux mixture to boiling stock and mix well. Lower heat to a slow simmer and cook 10 more minutes. Add hot sauce and cayenne pepper.

To serve, place 2–3 tablespoons of rice in a bowl then pour the hot gumbo over the rice.

Yield: 1 gallon

Shrimp Stock

2 pounds shrimp heads and shells, rinsed well and dried
½ cup cottonseed oil
½ pound yellow onion, peeled and medium dice
⅓ pound carrots, peeled and sliced thin
⅓ pound celery, cleaned and sliced thin
⅓ cup tomato paste
1 cup white wine
2 bay leaves
¼ bunch fresh parsley
4–6 sprigs thyme
1 tablespoon cracked black pepper
2 cloves garlic, crushed
1 gallon cold water

Preheat oven to 400°. Dry the shrimp shells as much as possible to prevent splattering.

Place oil in the largest ovenproof skillet in your kitchen and turn the heat to high. (You may set off your smoke alarm making this stock, but that's okay.) Put the shrimp shells in the oil and let them sit for 1–2 minutes (stirring will cool down the skillet). The shells should turn a coral-pink-brown-color. Stir 2 or 3 times until all shells have achieved this color.

Turn the heat down to medium and add the vegetables. Cook for 6–10 minutes, stirring occasionally. Add the tomato paste and stir it in to coat the vegetables. Place this mixture in the oven for 10 mintes. Remove from the oven and place all ingredients into a large stockpot.

Deglaze the skillet with the wine. Add this to the stockpot. Cover the mixture with cold water. Add the fresh herbs and bring to a medium simmer. Do not boil.

Cook for 2–3 hours—you will have to taste it to decide if it is done. If you are able to use a lot of shrimp heads, and not just shells, you will achieve a more intensely flavored stock sooner. Strain and cool.

Yield: 3 quarts

Mardi Gras Brunch Casserole

I love breakfast casseroles. They are perfect when you have friends or relatives visiting for the weekend. They can be made the night before, they're easy, they're quick, and they're good.

1 pound spicy andouille sausage, cut into ½-inch dice
¾ cup onion, diced
¼ cup green bell pepper, sliced
¼ cup red bell pepper, sliced
1 teaspoon garlic
1 teaspoon Creole Seasoning (recipe page 21)
1 teaspoon cayenne pepper
10 eggs, beaten
1 cup half-and-half
1 teaspoon dry mustard
5 croissants
¼ cup soft butter
1 cup smoked cheddar cheese, shredded
1 cup pepper jack cheese, shredded
1 teaspoon hot sauce

Preheat oven to 325°.

Brown sausage in a large skillet and drain most of the fat. Add onion, bell pepper, garlic, and seasoning and cook 5 minutes. Set aside.

Combine the eggs, half-and-half, and dry mustard in a mixing bowl. Spread the softened butter on both sides of each croissant. Cut the croissants into small cubes.

Fold the bread, cheeses, and sausage mixture into the eggs. Mix well and place in a buttered 2-quart baking dish.

Bake for 35–45 minutes. Allow to rest for 15 minutes before serving.

Yield: 8–10 servings

Grillades and Grits

A New Orleans brunch staple. Beef top round is a good substitute for when veal isn't available.

½ cup bacon grease (or canola oil)
2 pounds veal top round, cut into 2-inch strips
1 tablespoon black pepper, freshly ground, separated
2 teaspoons kosher salt, separated
¾ cup flour
¾ cup onion, diced
¼ cup shallot, minced
½ cup celery, diced
¾ cup green bell pepper, diced
½ teaspoon dried thyme
1 teaspoon garlic, minced
3 cups chicken broth, hot
½ cup red wine
1 bay leaf
1 cup tomatoes, peeled, large dice
2 teaspoons hot sauce

Place 1–2 tablespoons of the bacon grease in a large heavy skillet and place on high heat. Season meat with 1 teaspoon of the freshly ground pepper and 1 teaspoon of the kosher salt. Place the meat in hot skillet. Brown on all sides and remove from skillet.

Place remainder of the bacon grease into skillet. Once melted, lower heat and slowly stir in flour. Cook 3–4 minutes.

Add onion, shallot, celery, pepper, thyme, and garlic. Continue to cook roux mixture for 4–5 minutes. Using a wire whisk stir in the hot chicken broth, red wine, bay leaf, and tomatoes and bring to a simmer.

Add veal back to the mixture and cook over a very low heat for 2–3 hours, stirring occasionally. When meat is tender stir in hot sauce and the remaining black pepper and kosher salt.

Prepare Andouille-Cheese Grits (recipe follows) during the last 30 minutes of cooking. Spoon grits onto a serving dish and top with grillades.

Yield: 8–10 servings

ANDOUILLE CHEESE GRITS

1 tablespoon bacon fat or clarified butter

½ pound andouille sausage, medium dice

2 teaspoons garlic

4 cups milk

1 teaspoon salt

¼ teaspoon cayenne pepper

2 tablespoons hot sauce

2 tablespoons Creole Seasoning (recipe page 21)

½ cup unsalted butter

1 cup white grits, quick cooking

1 cup cheddar cheese, grated

In a large skillet, heat bacon fat or clarified butter until hot. Add andouille and garlic and sauté for 4–5 minutes. Remove from heat and drain off excess fat using a fine mesh strainer. Set the andouille-garlic mixture aside.

In a large saucepan, bring the milk, seasonings, and butter to a boil. Slowly pour in grits while stirring constantly. Reduce heat to low. Continue to stir for 15 minutes. Add the sautéed andouille and garlic mix, and cheese. Serve immediately.

Yield: 8–10 servings

Heart-Shaped Box

This box is meant for a special someone. In grade school we gave obligatory cards to the entire class so no one would feel left out. But, when everybody is special, no one is special.

King Cake Bread Pudding

In the Crescent City Grill we use a plain cream cheese King Cake when making this recipe. But if you are a fan of lemon or blueberry King Cake, feel free to substitute them.

2 cups milk
2 cups heavy whipping cream
¾ cup sugar, divided
4 egg yolks
8 eggs
2 teaspoons vanilla extract
⅛ teaspoon salt
1 teaspoon cinnamon
1 8–10-inch round cream cheese–filled King Cake

Place the milk, cream, and half of the sugar in a small saucepan and place over medium heat. Bring this mixture to a simmer, stirring occasionally to prevent the sugar from burning. While the milk mixture is heating, place the remaining sugar, egg yolks, whole eggs, vanilla, salt, and cinnamon into a stainless steel mixing bowl. Using a wire whisk, beat the egg mixture until it become light yellow in color. Slowly begin adding the hot milk to the beaten eggs, whisking constantly to prevent the eggs from scrambling.

Cut the King Cake into 2-inch slices. Pour half of the custard into a 2-quart round Pyrex baking dish (9-inch diameter). Submerge the King Cake slices into the custard. Pour the remaining custard over the top. Cover and refrigerate over night.

Preheat oven to 325°.

Remove the covering from the refrigerated bread pudding and gently press down the King Cake so that the custard completely covers the surface. Cover the bread pudding with a piece of parchment paper, and then cover the paper with a piece of aluminum foil.

In a roasting pan large enough to hold the Pyrex dish, place 2 inches of hot water. Place the Pyrex dish in the water and bake for 40 minutes. Remove the foil and parchment paper and bake for 10 additional minutes.

Remove from the oven and allow the pudding to rest for 1 hour. Serve with Brandy Crème Anglais (recipe follows).

Yield: 8–10 servings

BRANDY CRÈME ANGLAISE

1 cup cream
½ cup half-and-half
¼ cup brandy
¾ cup sugar, divided
1 teaspoon vanilla extract
4 egg yolks

In a stainless steel pot bring the cream, half-and-half, brandy, half of the sugar, and the vanilla to a simmer. While the mixture is heating, combine the yolks and remaining sugar in a mixing bowl and whip until pale yellow in color. Slowly begin adding the cream mixture into the yolks, stirring constantly until all the cream mixture has been added. Pour the mixture back into the saucepan and cook over a low-medium flame, stirring constantly, until the mixture becomes thick enough to coat a spoon or spatula. Remove from the heat and cool down in an ice bath.

This sauce may be made 2-3 days in advance.
Yields: 8–10 servings

Easter Lunch

Hearts of Palm and Artichoke Salad

Leg of Lamb with Raspberry Mint Chutney

Morel and Truffle Risotto

Asparagus Bread Pudding

Cheddar, Chive, and Black Pepper Biscuits

Caramel Cake

I Am the Egg Man

Easter was the holiday brought to us by a giant rabbit. We woke to find our candy, dressed up for church, and went to hear the preacher. A full morning. John Lennon said it best, "Goo goo ga joob."

Hearts of Palm
and Artichoke Salad

Make this recipe a few minutes in advance. The lettuce will wilt slightly, but the flavors imparted will be worth the trade off. The Garlic Croutons can be used in all types of salads.

SALAD DRESSING

1 tablespoon Dijon mustard

1 teaspoon sugar

1 tablespoon shallots, minced

3 tablespoons balsamic vinegar

¼ cup cottonseed oil

½ cup virgin olive oil

1 teaspoon fresh black pepper

1 teaspoon kosher salt

1 tablespoon fresh basil

1 cup tomato, finely diced

Place all ingredients into a mixing bowl and blend together using a wire whisk. Refrigerate until needed. This dressing will hold for 4–5 days refrigerated.

GARLIC CROUTONS

½ cup olive oil

1 tablespoon fresh garlic, minced

3 cups French bread cubes (1-inch)

½ tablespoon kosher salt

Preheat oven to 250°.

Place the oil in a small sauté pan over low heat. Add garlic to the warm oil and cook 2 minutes. Place bread cubes into a large mixing bowl and drizzle garlic oil over the bread. Toss bread several times making sure all bread is covered with the oil. Place croutons on a baking sheet and sprinkle kosher salt over them. Bake 10 minutes. Gently turn the croutons on the baking sheet and bake for another 15 minutes. Remove from oven and cool.

SALAD

2 14-ounce cans hearts of palm, sliced ¼-inch on a bias
2 12-ounce jars marinated artichoke hearts, drained
1 cup red onion, thinly shaved
3 cups romaine lettuce cut into thin pieces
¾ cup Romano cheese, shredded, divided
3 cups Garlic Croutons

Place the hearts of palm, artichoke hearts, red onion, romaine lettuce, half of the cheese, and the croutons in a large mixing bowl. Pour the dressing into the bowl and toss the ingredients with the dressing, making sure to coat everything completely. Place in a large serving bowl or on individual serving plates and top with the remaining Romano cheese. Serve immediately.

Yield: 8 servings

Leg of Lamb with Raspberry Mint Chutney

My grandmother roasted a leg of lamb one Sunday each month during my childhood. As a kid I wouldn't eat lamb. To get me to eat lamb, my mother would tell me it was roast beef. For the first eight years of my life I ate lamb thinking it was roast beef. Early on they told me that turkey was chicken, too. It's amazing that I ended up in the food business without a confused palate.

1 leg of lamb, bone in, about 6–7 pounds
12 cloves fresh garlic
¼ cup olive oil
1 tablespoon fresh rosemary, chopped
1 tablespoon fresh thyme, chopped
3 tablespoons kosher salt
1 tablespoon black pepper, freshly ground

Preheat oven to 375°.

Using a paring knife, cut 12 small pockets, spread out in the lamb leg. Insert 1 clove of garlic into each pocket. Rub the leg with the olive oil, then rub the herbs, salt, and pepper over the leg.

Place the lamb in a large roasting pan. Roast for 30 minutes, then reduce the heat to 325° and continue to bake for 1 hour and 15 minutes to achieve a medium rare temperature. If using a thermometer, it should register 145°.

Remove from the oven and allow the lamb to rest for 10 minutes. Slice thinly around the bone and serve.

Yield: Feeds one hungry family with several guests and a few disinherited cousins

RASPBERRY MINT CHUTNEY

1 tablespoon olive oil
½ cup shallots, minced
1 tablespoon garlic, minced
1 tablespoon fresh ginger, minced fine
2 teaspoons curry powder
¼ teaspoon black pepper, freshly ground
½ cup sherry

Yard Hand

Nurseries were not always popularly available. We grew our own flowers from seeds. My favorite was the Zinnia or Old Maid.

3 cups raspberries, fresh or frozen
1 cinnamon stick
2 cups chicken broth
1 bay leaf
1 cup mint jelly
1 teaspoon cornstarch
2 teaspoons water
½ teaspoon balsamic vinegar
1 tablespoon fresh mint, chopped

In a small saucepan, heat olive oil over medium-high heat and cook shallots 3–4 minutes. Stir in garlic, ginger, curry powder, and pepper and cook 3–4 more minutes, stirring often. Do not let garlic brown. Deglaze with sherry and reduce by half.

Stir in 2 cups of the raspberries, the cinnamon stick, and the chicken broth, and bay leaf and simmer 15–20 minutes, until reduced by half. Stir in mint jelly and cook 3 minutes more, stirring constantly. Dissolve the cornstarch with the 2 teaspoons of water and stir it into the simmering sauce. Allow the sauce to thicken then remove from heat and strain. Stir in the vinegar, fresh mint, and remaining cup of raspberries.

Serve at room temperature.

Yield: 2 cups

Morel and Truffle Risotto

Risotto refers to the cooking method (slowly adding stock), not the rice. Arborio rice is the variety most often used. Don't be afraid of risotto. It's easy, it just takes time.

3 tablespoons + 2 tablespoons unsalted butter
3 tablespoons shallots, minced
2 cups Aborio rice, uncooked
4–6 cups hot mushroom stock
1 tablespoon salt, added to the mushroom stock
¾ ounce dry morels, or 3 ounces fresh, sliced ¼-inch (if using dry, cover the mushrooms completely with hot water, soak until softened, and then slice)
1 cup cream
½ cup Parmesan cheese, freshly grated
2 tablespoons fresh parsley, chopped
2 teaspoons fresh thyme, chopped
1 teaspoon black pepper, freshly ground
2 tablespoons truffle oil

In a very large skillet, heat 3 tablespoons of butter over medium heat and add shallots. Cook until onions become soft. Add rice. Stir constantly to prevent rice from browning. The grains of rice need to get hot. Add 1½ cups of stock and turn heat down so that the stock is barely simmering. As the stock is absorbed, add more stock in small amounts, stirring constantly. Continue this process until the grains become slightly tender.

In a separate skillet, place the other 2 tablespoons of butter over medium heat. Add sliced mushrooms and sauté until soft. Add the mushrooms to the risotto. When rice is almost completely cooked, add the cream and again stir until absorbed. Remove from heat and stir in cheese, fresh herbs, and pepper.

Drizzle the truffle oil over the risotto just before serving. Serve immediately.
Yield: 6–8 servings

Asparagus Bread Pudding

I ate a version of this at Blackberry Farm, a beautiful and quaint little resort in the foothills of the Smoky Mountains. My adaptation, like Blackberry Farm's, is a very elegant and flavorful accompaniment to any dinner or formal lunch.

3 cups water
1 cup asparagus cut into 1-inch pieces
1 tablespoon olive oil
½ cup white onion, diced
½ cup red pepper, diced
1 teaspoon salt
1 teaspoon black pepper, freshly ground
½ cup Riesling wine
12 tablespoons fresh basil, chopped
1 teaspoon dry mustard
1 cup sour cream
1 cup half-and-half
½ cup whole milk
4 egg yolks
2 eggs
6 cups French bread, crust removed, small diced

Place 3 cups of water into a small saucepan and bring to a boil. Place the asparagus pieces in the boiling water and cook for 45 seconds. Strain the asparagus and shock it in an ice bath or run it under cold water until cooled completely. Drain and dry the asparagus pieces and set aside.

In a medium sauté pan, heat the oil over medium heat. Sauté the onions and peppers for 2–3 minutes. Add the cooked asparagus, salt, and pepper and cook for 1 minute more. Add the wine and allow it to reduce by half. Remove this mixture from the heat and set aside.

In a large mixing bowl, combine the basil, dry mustard, sour cream, half-and-half, milk, and eggs. Blend together and fold in the cooked vegetables and French bread. Cover and allow the mixture to set for 1 hour before baking.

Preheat oven to 325°.

Place the pudding mixture into a lightly buttered 2-quart Pyrex baking dish. Cover the pudding with a piece of parchment paper, and cover the parchment paper with a piece of aluminum foil. Bake for 35 minutes covered. Remove the foil and paper and cook for an additional 10 minutes. Allow pudding to rest for 10 minutes before serving.

Yield: 8–10 servings

For Purple Martins Majesty

In the deep South the swallows don't return as they do to Capistrano, but Purple Martins come back every year to enjoy their fill of bugs and keep the neighborhood mosquito free.

Cheddar, Chive, and Black Pepper Biscuits

Purple Parrot chef Linda Nance created these biscuits several years ago. They remain one of the staples in our bread basket. Freezing and grating the butter are the secrets to light and fluffy biscuits. The butter steams inside the biscuit as it cooks. Never overmix or the biscuits will be hard and tough.

2 cups flour
1 tablespoon sugar
1½ teaspoons baking soda
1 teaspoon baking powder
1 tablespoon kosher salt
2 teaspoons black pepper, freshly ground
½ cup cheddar cheese, shredded
2 tablespoons chives, chopped
½ cup frozen butter
¾ cup + 2 tablespoons buttermilk
1 egg
3 tablespoons unsalted butter, melted

Preheat oven to 375°.

In a large mixing bowl, combine the flour, sugar, baking soda, baking powder, salt, pepper, cheddar cheese, and chives. Gently mix to combine the ingredients.

Using a cheese grater, carefully shred the frozen butter into the flour mixture. Lightly toss to incorporate. Work fast as it is very important to keep butter as cold as possible.

In a separate bowl, whisk together the buttermilk and egg.

Add the buttermilk mixture to the flour mixture, and using your hands, blend the dough. Blend only long enough to moisten all of the flour. Do not overmix.

Place the biscuit dough on a lightly floured surface and roll out to ¾-inch thickness. Cut biscuits using a 2–inch round cookie cutter (do not twist when cutting, use a straight and quick up and down motion).

Place biscuits on a cookie sheet. Using a pastry brush, brush the tops with the melted butter. Bake 12–14 minutes.

Yield: 10–14 biscuits

Caramel Cake

A local baker in my hometown named Cora Eckstein makes the world's best caramel cake. This is not her recipe, but a good one nonetheless. Patience and a candy thermometer are a must. The cake is best when served at room temperature.

CAKE

2½ cups cake flour
2 teaspoons baking soda
1 teaspoon baking powder
½ teaspoon kosher salt
2 eggs
2 cups sugar
¾ cup melted butter
1 cup buttermilk
1 cup milk
1 teaspoon vanilla extract

Preheat oven to 350°.

Lightly butter 2 8-inch cake pans and line with parchment. Butter the parchment and flour the pans, shaking out the excess.

Sift together flour, baking soda, baking powder, and salt.
In a mixer with a whip attachment, beat eggs and sugar until thick and lemon-colored. Beat in the melted butter. Alternately add dry ingredients with buttermilk, milk, and vanilla, scraping the bowl once or twice to form a thin batter. Divide between prepared cake pans.

Bake until a toothpick inserted in the center of the cake comes out clean, 40–45 minutes. Cool in pan for 15 minutes. Invert onto cooling racks, peel off paper, and cool completely. Once the cakes have cooled completely, use a sharp knife to cut each layer in half, creating 4 thin layers of cake.

CARAMEL FROSTING

4 cups firmly packed brown sugar
2 cups whipping cream
½ cup unsalted butter
2 teaspoons vanilla extract

Combine the brown sugar and cream in a heavy-duty 3-quart saucepan. Bring to a boil and cook until the mixture reaches softball stage (234°–238° on a candy thermometer). Stir frequently during this stage to prevent burning. Remove from the heat.

Using an electric mixer, blend the butter and vanilla. Slowly add the cream mixture. Continue beating until the icing becomes thick enough to spread. This process takes 10–15 minutes, so be patient.

If the frosting becomes too thick to spread, beat in a few drops of very hot water. Spread a little less than ¼ of the frosting over the top of one cake layer. Place the next layer atop the iced layer, and repeat the icing process until all layers have been iced. Spread remaining icing around the sides of the cake.

Yield: 10–14 servings

Endless Summer

Give someone a fish and he eats for a day. Give someone a rod and reel and he fishes all day.

Light Spring Lunch

Pesto Pasta with Roasted Portobello Mushroom
Strips and Asparagus

Tobacco Onion Caesar Salad

Roasted Garlic Parmesan Bread

Golden Pineapple Sorbet with a Minted Cookie

White Bloomers
Gardenias bring to mind
Vacation Bible School and summer
holidays. The fragrance is one of my
fondest childhood memories. I don't
remember the dogma as much as the
crafts projects, KoolAid, and cheap
cookies.

Pesto Pasta with Roasted Portobello Mushroom Strips and Asparagus

This is easy and flavorful and is a great recipe to make when entertaining. My kids love it for supper, too. The gills on the underside of the mushrooms can become tough and bitter when cooked. They are easily removed by gently scraping the underside of the mushroom with a teaspoon.

PORTOBELLOS

1 cup Creamy Balsamic Dressing (recipe page 28)
2 teaspoons garlic, minced
½ cup vegetable broth
2 teaspoons creole mustard
1 teaspoon hot sauce
2 teaspoons Creole Seasoning (recipe page 21)
1 teaspoon black pepper, freshly ground
2 teaspoons Worcestershire sauce
5–6 fresh portobello mushrooms, stems and gills removed

Combine the first 8 ingredients in a mixing bowl. Dip each portobello mushroom in the mixture to coat it completely. Refrigerate for 1 hour.

Preheat oven to 350°.

After the mushrooms have marinated, place them on a baking sheet with the top side down. Cover the baking sheet completely with aluminum foil and bake for 7 minutes. Remove the foil and bake for 5 more minutes. Allow the mushrooms to cool, then cut them into ¾-inch-wide strips.

ASPARAGUS

1 pound asparagus, fresh
2 tablespoons olive oil
1 teaspoon salt
½ teaspoon pepper
2 tablespoons toasted, slivered almonds

Preheat oven to 350°.

Toss the asparagus with olive oil, salt, and pepper. Place on baking sheet lined with wax paper. Bake 12 minutes. Remove from oven and sprinkle the almonds over the asparagus.

PESTO

3 cups loosely packed basil leaves, washed and dried very well
⅓ cup pine nuts
¼ cup Parmigiano Reggiano, freshly grated
1 tablespoon garlic, minced
1 teaspoon kosher salt
½ cup extra virgin olive oil

In a food processor, combine and puree the basil, pine nuts, cheese, garlic, and salt. With the processor still running, slowly drizzle in the olive oil. Remove the lid and scrape down the sides of the processor to make sure there are no large pieces of basil. Puree for another 30–40 seconds. Use immediately or refrigerate covered with plastic for up to 4 days. The plastic wrap should be placed directly on the surface of the pesto to prevent discoloration. Pesto make also be frozen in an airtight container and held for 1 month.

PASTA

1 pound spaghetti, linguini, or bowtie pasta
2 tablespoons unsalted butter
Roasted Portobello Mushroom Strips
¼ cup chicken or vegetable broth, or pasta water
¾ cup fresh pesto
½ teaspoon salt
¼ teaspoon pepper, freshly ground
¾ cup Parmigiano Reggiano cheese, coarsely grated

Cook the pasta according to the directions on the package.

In a large sauté pan, melt the butter over medium heat. Place the cooked mushrooms in the pan and heat for 3–4 minutes. Add the broth, pesto, salt, and pepper. Place in a large stainless steel bowl.

Add the cooked pasta to the bowl and mix well, making sure that the pasta is evenly coated with the pesto and mushrooms.

Arrange 6–8 asparagus spears on each serving plate creating a star pattern with the base of the stalks in the center of the plate and the tips of the spears pointing outward toward the edge of the plate. Divide the pesto-coated pasta onto the serving dishes, over the asparagus, and sprinkle with the shredded Parmigiano Reggiano cheese. Serve immediately.

Yield: 4–6 servings

Tobacco Onion Caesar Salad

The Caesar dressing is best when prepared a few days ahead. The tobacco onions must be cooked at the last minute.

DRESSING

2 egg yolks
¼ cup fresh lemon juice
2 tablespoons fresh garlic, minced
3 anchovies
2 tablespoons red wine vinegar
1 tablespoon Worcestershire sauce
2 tablespoons Dijon mustard
1 cup light olive oil

Combine the yolks, lemon juice, garlic, anchovies, vinegar, Worcestershire sauce, and Dijon mustard in a blender or small food processor. Puree for 1–2 minutes. While the blender is running, slowly drizzle in the olive oil. If the mixture becomes too thick, add 1–2 tablespoons of warm water, and continue to add the oil. Store refrigerated until ready to use.

GARLIC CROUTONS

2 cups French bread cut into ½-inch cubes
3 tablespoons olive oil
2 teaspoons garlic powder
½ teaspoon kosher salt

Preheat oven to 275°.

Place the cubed bread into a mixing bowl and drizzle the olive oil over the bread. Sprinkle the garlic powder over the bread and toss the uncooked croutons well, evenly distributing the oil and garlic. Place the cubed bread on a baking sheet and toast for 8–12 minutes, stirring every 3 minutes. Remove from the oven and sprinkle with kosher salt. Allow croutons to cool completely. Store in an airtight container until needed.

Studying Each Other
In the spring a young man's fancy lightly turns to love. This couple is studying poetry on the grass in front of Locksley Hall.

TOBACCO ONIONS

1 large red onion, shaved into very thin circles (about 1¼ cups)
2 tablespoons white vinegar
½ tablespoon kosher salt
⅛ teaspoon black pepper, freshly ground
1 quart vegetable oil for frying
½ cup milk
1 whole egg
1½ cups seasoned flour (1½ cups flour and 3 tablespoons Creole Seasoning, recipe page 21)

Combine the onion, vinegar, salt, and pepper in a medium mixing bowl and marinate 30 minutes.

Heat oil to 350° in a 6-quart heavy-duty saucepan, or a large cast iron skillet.

Whisk together milk and egg in a mixing bowl. Place onions in the milk mixture and drain well.

Place seasoned flour in another mixing bowl and toss onions in the flour, making sure onions are all well coated with flour. Remove onions from the bowl and shake off excess flour.

Place breaded onions in the hot oil and, using a slotted spoon, gently turn them once or twice. Fry for 3–4 minutes. Remove the onions and place them on a paper towel–lined baking sheet to drain.

FOR THE SALAD

3 romaine hearts or 1 large head of romaine, washed and thoroughly dried, outer leaves
    discarded
2 cups Garlic Croutons
1½ cups Caesar salad dressing
Tobacco Onions
½ cup Parmesan cheese, freshly grated

Place the clean lettuce in a large mixing bowl. Add the croutons and dressing and mix well, making sure the lettuce is well coated. Gently fold in half of the tobacco onions. Divide the salad onto serving plates. Use the remaining tobacco onions to top each salad. Sprinkle with Parmesan cheese and serve immediately.

Yield: 6–8 servings

Roasted Garlic Parmesan Bread

My daughter says "Daddy, that bread is the bomb-dot-com." Purple Parrot Café Chef Linda Nance says it's the best garlic bread she's ever eaten. I say, pass me another piece.

ROASTED GARLIC PUREE

2 whole heads of garlic
¼ cup olive oil
2 teaspoons kosher salt

Preheat oven to 350°.

Remove the outermost layers of skin on the garlic heads. Cut the top off so that the cloves are exposed and place—exposed side up—in a shallow baking dish. Heat the olive oil over high heat for 1–2 minutes. Stir salt into the oil and pour the oil directly over the tops of the garlic. Cover garlic with foil and bake 30 minutes. Remove the foil and bake for an additional 8 minutes.

Remove from the oven and cool the garlic. To remove the roasted garlic cloves, gently squeeze the bottom of the head and the garlic should slide out easily. Place the roasted garlic cloves on a cutting board and, using the flat side of a chef's knife, smash the garlic into a puree.

Yield: ¼ + cup garlic puree

BREAD

½ cup unsalted butter, room temperature
¼ cup Roasted Garlic Puree
2 teaspoons fresh parsley, chopped
1 teaspoon fresh chives, sliced very thin
¼ teaspoon kosher salt
¼ teaspoon Creole Seasoning (recipe page 21)
½ teaspoon Worcestershire sauce
¼ teaspoon black pepper, freshly ground
½ cup Parmigiano-Reggiano, freshly grated (about 2 ounces ungrated), separated
1 French baguette (12–14 inches long), cut in half lengthwise

Preheat oven to 350°.

Cream together the softened butter, Roasted Garlic Puree, herbs, salt, Creole Seasoning, Worcestershire sauce, pepper, and half of the cheese, using a rubber spatula or wooden spoon. Spread both halves of the baguette evenly with the butter mixture. Sprinkle the remaining cheese on top of the butter mixture.

Line a large baking sheet with aluminum foil and place the prepared halves, butter side up, on the baking sheet. Bake for 12–15 minutes. Cut crosswise on a diagonal into 1½-inch slices. Serve immediately.

Yield: 8–10 servings

Golden Pineapple Sorbet
with a Minted Cookie

Golden pineapple is much sweeter than the standard variety. Add freshly chopped mint to the sorbet for an extra flavor dimension. Canned pineapple may be substituted when good-quality fresh is not available (premium canned pineapple is better than bad, over-ripe, fresh pineapple).

½ cup water
¾ cup sugar
¼ cup Karo syrup
1 tablespoon fresh lemon juice
1 large ripe Golden pineapple, rind and core removed, and cubed (approximately 5 cups)

Make a simple syrup by placing the water and sugar in a small saucepan and heating until the sugar is completely dissolved. Allow the syrup to cool completely.

Place the simple syrup, Karo syrup, lemon juice, and pineapple in a blender. On high speed, puree the mixture until it is smooth. Strain the mixture through a fine strainer and refrigerate for 1 hour.

Following the manufacturer's directions, freeze the liquid using an electric ice cream machine. Remove from the ice cream maker and store, covered, in the freezer for 2 hours before serving. The sorbet may be held in the freezer for 1 week.

Yield: 1 quart

MINTED COOKIE

½ cup butter
¼ cup sugar
1 medium egg
½ teaspoon mint extract
1 teaspoon vanilla extract
1½ cups flour
¼ teaspoon baking powder
10 peppermints, crushed

Preheat oven to 350°.

Cream butter and sugar; beat in egg and mint and vanilla extracts. Sift flour and baking powder together and stir into mixture. Refrigerate 1 hour, or until dough is firm enough to roll. On a floured surface, roll to ⅛-inch thickness and cut with cookie cutters. Sprinkle the tops with the crushed peppermint pieces. Bake 10–12 minutes.

Yield: 12–16 cookies

waters

Seafood Supper
at the Beach

West Indies Crab Salad
with French Bread Croutons

Roasted Silver Queen Corn and Shrimp Dip

Crab Bread with Tomato Basil Concasse

Paneed Red Snapper with Creole Cream Sauce,
Mushrooms, and Crawfish

Creole Cream Sauce

Fresh Strawberries with Crème Anglaise

Bloody Mary Oyster Shooters

Destined for Greatness
Why we vacation in the heat of
the summer to an even hotter
place is a mystery to me. The lure of
water is universal. We love to make
the pilgrimage, regardless of the
inconvenience, just to say
we have been.

PAGES 66–67:
Both Sides Now
Who doesn't like looking at clouds
and letting his or her mind drift from
one image to another. I know I have
found my pace when I can see a cloud
slowly change from a '42 Plymouth
to a duck.

West Indies Crab Salad with French Bread Croutons

A staple of my youth. My family had a small fish camp on the Gulf Coast. In the summers we'd catch dozens of fresh crab, bring them back to the camp, and boil them, just minutes out of the water. We made several dishes with the freshly picked crabmeat, but West Indies Salad was always one of them.

2 pounds jumbo lump crabmeat
1½ cups yellow onion, small dice
½ cup canola, cottonseed, or peanut oil
½ cup champagne vinegar
¼ cup ice water
2 tablespoons fresh parsley, chopped
1 tablespoon plus 1 teaspoon kosher salt
1 teaspoon black pepper, freshly ground

Gently fold all ingredients together and cover tightly. Refrigerate overnight before serving. Just before serving, toss the salad well to redistribute the dressing.

FRENCH BREAD CROUTONS

2 French baguettes, sliced into 1-inch-thick rounds
⅔ cups light olive oil
3 garlic cloves, peeled
½ tablespoon kosher salt

Preheat oven to 400°.

Arrange the sliced bread on 1 large baking sheet. Use a pastry brush to brush each slice of bread with the olive oil.

Bake for 4–5 minutes. Remove the bread from the oven and quickly rub each slice with the raw garlic. Sprinkle with the kosher salt and serve.

Yield: 6–8 servings

Pail by Comparison
There is a parable about someone who built his house on a rock and another who built his house on sand. I think the one on sand would have been a lot more fun.

Roasted Silver Queen Corn and Shrimp Dip

My wife makes a version of this when we entertain in the summertime. Adjust the heat to your liking, or go easy on the cayenne and place a bottle of hot sauce next to the bowl of dip.

2 quarts water
1 tablespoon crab boil
2 tablespoons kosher salt
¾ pound small shrimp, head on
½ cup sour cream
½ cup mayonnaise
¼ cup red onion, minced
½ cup green onion, minced
1 tablespoon fresh jalapeño, minced
1 tablespoon hot sauce
1 tablespoon fresh lime juice
⅛ teaspoon cayenne pepper
¼ teaspoon ground cumin
⅓ cup fresh cilantro, chopped
1½ cups roasted Silver Queen corn cut from the cob* (3 ears)
1 teaspoon salt

Bring the water, crab boil, and salt to a boil over high heat. Add shrimp to the boiling water and reduce heat. Simmer the shrimp for 6–8 minutes. Remove from heat and drain shrimp. Place the cooked shrimp in the refrigerator and cool completely. Peel and roughly chop the cooled shrimp. Combine shrimp and the remaining ingredients in a large mixing bowl and mix well. Refrigerate for 1–2 hours before serving. Serve with your favorite chips for dipping.

Yield: 6–8 servings

*To roast the corn: Preheat oven to 375°. Wrap each ear individually in aluminum foil and place it on a baking sheet. Cook for 15 minutes. Turn each piece of corn over and bake for 15 more minutes. Remove from the oven and cool for 30 minutes. Remove the foil, husks, and silk, and using a sharp knife, cut the kernels from the corn, being careful not to cut too deeply into the cob. Allow corn to cool completely before preparing the dip.

Crab Bread with Tomato Basil Concasse

An often requested feature at the Crescent City Grill. Make sure to let the bread rest for five minutes after it comes out of the oven.

3 tablespoon butter, separated
2 tablespoons green onions, thinly sliced
¼ cup red peppers, diced
1 teaspoon salt
¼ teaspoon black pepper, freshly ground
2 tablespoons flour
⅓ cup hot chicken stock
2 tablespoons sherry
1 teaspoon lemon juice
1 tablespoon hot sauce
½ pound cream cheese, softened
½ cup Swiss cheese, grated
½ pound fresh lump crabmeat
2 tablespoons parsley, chopped
1 French baguette, 16–20 inches in length

Preheat oven to 375°.

Melt the first tablespoon of butter in a small sauté pan over a medium heat. Add the green onions, peppers, salt, and pepper and cook 1 minute. Remove from the heat and set aside.

Melt the remaining 2 tablespoons of butter in a small sauté pan over low heat. Stir in the flour to form a roux. Cook the roux for 3–4 minutes, stirring constantly. Be careful not to burn the roux. Whisk the hot stock, sherry, lemon juice, and hot sauce into the roux mixture. Cook 3–4 minutes more and remove from heat.

Using an electric mixer with a paddle attachment, place the softened cream cheese into the bowl and beat for 2–3 minutes. Scrape the sides of the bowl using a rubber spatula, and add the thickened stock mixture, peppers and onions, and Swiss cheese. Blend until smooth. Using a rubber spatula, gently fold in the crab and parsley.

Cut the baguette in half lengthwise and spread the crab mixture evenly over the bread. Place the 2 halves on a foil-lined baking sheet and bake 20 minutes. Remove the bread from the oven and allow to cool 3–4 minutes. Using a sharp serrated knife, cut bread into 2-inch slices. Arrange slices on a serving dish and top each piece with a teaspoon of Tomato Basil Concasse (recipe follows).

TOMATO BASIL CONCASSE

1½ cups fresh ripe tomatoes, seeds removed, very small dice
½ teaspoon garlic, minced
½ teaspoon salt
⅛ teaspoon black pepper, freshly ground
1 tablespoon orange juice, freshly squeezed
¼ cup fresh basil, chopped
2 tablespoons extra virgin olive oil

Combine all ingredients.
    Yield: 8 servings

Salted and Unsalted
Swimming in a small pool next to
a large body of water is a popular
summer pastime. The smell of chlorine
still makes me think of sunburns and
the color aqua.

Paneed Red Snapper with Creole Cream Sauce, Mushrooms, and Crawfish

A versatile sauce that works well with pasta, shrimp, and chicken. Pack a pint in an ice chest for use in multiple applications when you travel on your beach vacation.

1 cup seasoned flour (1 cup flour to 3 tablespoons Creole Seasoning, recipe page 21)
8 red snapper filets, 6–8 ounces each
4 tablespoons clarified butter, divided
4 cups sliced button mushrooms
1 tablespoon garlic, minced
1½ cups green onion, sliced
3 ounces white wine
1½ cups Creole Cream Sauce (recipe follows)
1 pound crawfish tails, cooked and peeled
2 tablespoons fresh parsley, chopped

Preheat oven to 350°.

Place seasoned flour into a large shallow pan. Lightly dust the fish filets in the flour.

Heat half of the butter in a large sauté pan over medium-high heat and brown both sides of fish. Do not overload the sauté pan. Once the fish is browned, place filets on baking sheet and cook in oven for 5–10 minutes, depending upon the thickness of the filet.

Add the remaining butter to the sauté pan and sauté mushrooms until tender. Add garlic and green onions and cook 2–3 minutes more. Deglaze with white wine, allowing wine to reduce by half. Add the Creole Cream Sauce and simmer for 1–2 minutes. Stir in the crawfish and cook for 2 more minutes. Remove filets from oven and place on serving dishes. Evenly divide topping over fish and serve. Garnish with fresh parsley.

Yield: 6–8 servings

Creole Cream Sauce

2 cups heavy cream
1 tablespoon Creole Seasoning (recipe page 21)
2 tablespoons Worcestershire sauce
2 tablespoons hot sauce
1 teaspoon paprika

Place all ingredients in a double boiler over medium-high heat and reduce by one-half until thickened.

Ice Cube

Ice was once harvested, shipped in straw from up north, and then delivered to an "ice box" to chill food. Now bagged ice almost always means a party; that, or your refrigerator is broken.

Fresh Strawberries
with Crème Anglaise

If I could only eat one dessert for the rest of my life, this would be it. Fruit, not chocolate, is my favorite choice to finish a meal. This is good for breakfast, too. Along with strawberries, blackberries, blueberries, raspberries, or any combination of the four work well. I take a quart of the Crème Anglaise when I go on a beach vacation and purchase fresh berries once we arrive. Serve raspberries and blueberries with Crème Anglaise for a great red, white, and blue dessert on the Fourth of July.

1 cup cream
1 cup half-and-half
2 tablespoons Grand Marnier
2 teaspoons vanilla extract
¾ cup sugar, divided
5 egg yolks
4 pints fresh strawberries, hulls removed and berries quartered
½ cup sugar
1 tablespoon fresh lemon juice

In a 1-quart stainless steel pot bring the cream, half-and-half, Grand Marnier, vanilla, and half of the sugar to a simmer. While the cream mixture is heating, combine the yolks and remaining sugar in a mixing bowl and whip until light in color.

Slowly temper (pour) the cream mixture into the yolks. Once all of the cream has been added to the yolk mixture, return the mixture to the pot. Cook over low-medium heat, stirring constantly with a rubber spatula. Do not use a whip. Make sure to stir the edges and bottom of the saucepan well while the sauce is cooking. Cook the mixture until it becomes thick enough to coat a spoon or spatula.

Remove from the heat. Pour the sauce immediately into a stainless steel bowl and cool down over an ice bath. Refrigerate until needed. This sauce will hold for 3–4 days covered and refrigerated.

While the sauce is cooling, prepare the strawberries. Place the cleaned and cut berries in a large mixing bowl. Sprinkle the sugar and lemon juice over the berries and gently toss them in the bowl so that the sugar gets evenly distributed. Do this 1–2 hours before serving.

To serve, divide the strawberries evenly among 8 small chilled serving bowls or ice cream dishes. Drizzle ¼ cup of the sauce over the berries and serve.

Yield: 8 servings

Bloody Mary Oyster Shooters

These are usually the first to go at all of our catered events. Have backups ready because they go fast.

18 freshly shucked oysters

BLOODY MARY COCKTAIL SAUCE

1 cup ketchup
½ cup chili sauce
¼ cup V-8 juice
2 tablespoons + 1 teaspoon Worcestershire sauce
2 tablespoons lemon juice, freshly squeezed
2 tablespoons prepared horseradish
1½ tablespoons Tabasco
¼ teaspoon black pepper, freshly ground
½ teaspoon salt
1 teaspoon celery salt

One day in advance, prepare the cocktail sauce by combining all ingredients.

To serve, place 1 oyster in a shot glass. Top with 2 tablespoons of the cocktail sauce and serve.

Yield: 18 servings

Five-Course Midsummer Night Seafood Feast

Crabmeat Wontons with a Sweet
Chili Pepper Dipping Sauce

Fried Oyster Salad

Seafood Courtbouillon

Shrimp Harrison

Black Strap Molasses Muffins

Raspberry White Chocolate Bread Pudding

Lightning Bugs
Their bioluminescence attracts
mates and things to eat. The Chinese
captured fireflies in containers
and used them as a type of lantern
just like this.

Crabmeat Wontons with a Sweet Chili Pepper Dipping Sauce

At the Crescent City Grill, we serve over 1,200 of these each week. They might be tricky to prepare at home, but will be well worth the effort. A deep-fat thermometer is a must to maintain temperature when frying.

½ pound cream cheese, softened
1 teaspoon soy sauce
1 teaspoon hot sauce
⅛ teaspoon fresh ginger, finely minced
1 teaspoon Creole Seasoning (recipe page 21)
2 tablespoons green onions, very thinly sliced
½ pound fresh lump crabmeat
30–36 wonton skins
3 egg yolks
1–2 quarts vegetable oil for frying

Using the paddle attachment on an electric mixer, whip the cream cheese until light and fluffy, scraping the sides and bottom of the bowl several times to make sure all of the cream cheese gets whipped. Turn off the mixer and add soy sauce, hot sauce, ginger, and Creole Seasoning. Mix on medium speed until all ingredients are well blended, again scraping down the sides of the bowl several times. Remove the paddle attachment and gently fold in the green onions and crabmeat. Refrigerate the mixture for at least 2 hours before filling wontons. The filling may be made a day in advance.

To fill the wontons:
Lay 10–12 wonton skins on a flat surface and place 2–3 teaspoons of filling in the center of each wrapper. Using a pastry brush, lightly dampen the outer edges of the wrappers with egg yolk, but do not soak them. Firmly seal the outer edges together to form a semicircle. Place the finished wontons on a baking sheet lined with waxed paper. Continue this process until all wrappers have been filled. Place the finished wontons in the freezer until firm.

To fry:

Preheat oven to 200° and line a baking sheet with paper towels.

Heat the oil to 350° in a 8–10-quart heavy-duty saucepan, or a large cast-iron skillet. Gently place 10–12 wontons in the oil. Using a large slotted spoon, turn the wontons over to make sure both sides are browned. Cook wontons for approximately 5–7 minutes, or until both sides are golden brown. Remove the wontons using a slotted spoon and place on the towel-lined baking sheet. Hold the cooked wontons in the warm oven and continue cooking the remaining wontons.

Wontons may be made up to 2 weeks in advance and stored frozen. If freezing for a period of time, first allow the wontons to freeze uncovered on a baking sheet. When they are completely frozen, you may place them in an airtight container.

Yield: 30–36 wontons

SWEET CHILI PEPPER DIPPING SAUCE

1 cup water
¼ cup red chili pepper flakes
1 large red bell pepper, seeds removed
1 tablespoon garlic, minced
1 tablespoon fresh ginger, minced
½ cup rice vinegar
1 cup white wine vinegar
1 cup sugar
¾ cup corn syrup
2 tablespoons water
2 tablespoons cornstarch

Bring 1 cup of water to a boil in a small saucepan. Stir in chili flakes and simmer 5 minutes. Strain flakes, set aside, and discard water.

Place red bell pepper, garlic, and ginger in a small stainless steel saucepan with vinegars and simmer 5–6 minutes. Allow mixture to cool slightly, then puree in a blender. Return pureed mixture to the stainless steel pot and add sugar and corn syrup. Bring the mixture back to a simmer.

Dissolve cornstarch in 2 tablespoons of water and blend into the red pepper mixture. Once it returns to a simmer, remove from heat. Stir in the red pepper flakes and chill.

May be made 1 week in advance.

Yield: 3 cups

Fried Oyster Salad

The oysters must be fried crispy and never soggy. The temperature of the oil must be 350° and a deep-frying thermometer is a must to maintain an even temperature. The Comeback Sauce is a Mississippi-Greek restaurant staple and is good as a dip, condiment, or salad dressing.

COMEBACK SAUCE

1 cup mayonnaise
½ cup ketchup
½ cup chili sauce
½ cup cottonseed oil
½ cup yellow onion, grated
3 tablespoons lemon juice
2 tablespoons garlic, minced
1 tablespoon paprika
1 tablespoon water
1 tablespoon Worcestershire sauce
1 teaspoon pepper
½ teaspoon dry mustard
1 teaspoon salt

Combine all ingredients in a food processor and mix well.
  Yield: 3½ cups

FRIED OYSTERS

2 cups cornmeal
¾ cup corn flour
2 teaspoons salt
2 tablespoons + 1 teaspoon Creole Seasoning (recipe page 21)
32 oysters, freshly shucked
peanut oil for frying

Heat oil in cast-iron skillet to 350°.
    Combine cornmeal, corn flour, salt, and Creole Seasoning. Coat oysters with cornmeal mixture and drop one at a time into hot oil. Fry until golden and crispy (approximately 5 minutes). Remove from oil and drain on paper towels. Hold in a 200° oven for 3–5 minutes while completing the assembly of the salad.

Old Maids

Jerry Garcia wasn't the first. My grandmother taught me to dead head Zinnias so that they would continue to bloom. If you don't cut them they quit flowering and go to seed. They also look great in a vase.

TO ASSEMBLE THE SALAD:

4 cups iceberg lettuce cut into 2-inch squares
2 cups green leaf lettuce cut into 2-inch squares
1 cup red cabbage, shaved
⅓ cup roasted red bell pepper, small dice
½ cup bacon, cooked and chopped
1 cup Parmesan cheese grated into large shreds, divided
⅓ cup red onion, thinly shaved
4 hard-boiled eggs, chopped

Place both lettuces, shredded cabbage, red bell pepper, chopped bacon, and half of the Parmesan cheese in a large mixing bowl. Toss the lettuce mixture with 1½ cups of the Comeback Sauce. The lettuce should be lightly coated with the dressing. (If you feel that the salad needs more dressing, add another ½ cup.)

Divide the salad onto 8 serving plates. Top each salad with a small amount of the remaining Parmesan cheese, shaved red onion, and chopped egg. Place 4 fried oysters on each salad and serve immediately.

Serve the remaining Comeback Sauce in a side dish to be used as a dipping sauce for the oysters.

Yield: 8 servings

Seafood Courtbouillon

Redfish is used in the stock. If it is not available, use another mild-flavored fish such as snapper or grouper.

FISH STOCK

3 quarts water
1 cup white wine
1 cup yellow onion, medium dice
1 cup carrot, peeled and small dice
1 cup celery, small dice
4 bay leaves
1 tablespoon cracked black pepper
1 teaspoon dry thyme
¼ cup fresh parsley leaves
2 2-pound bone-in cleaned, redfish, head removed

Place the water and all ingredients except the fish in a large saucepan over medium heat. Bring to a simmer and place the fish in the water. Simmer for 10–15 minutes. Remove fish, allow to cool. Remove all the meat from the bones and reserve meat. Return the bones to the stock and continue simmering while making the roux.

COURTBOULLION

¾ cup oil
¾ cup flour
½ cup andouille, ¾-inch dice
1 cup yellow onion, medium dice
¾ cup celery, medium dice
¼ cup red bell pepper, medium dice
¼ cup green bell pepper, medium dice
2 quarts fish stock
2 tablespoons fresh garlic, minced
1 teaspoon dried basil
¼ teaspoon dry thyme
1 cup canned diced tomatoes
1 8-ounce can tomato sauce
1 8-ounce can Rotel tomatoes
2 bay leaves
1 cup chopped green onions
1 pound large shrimp, peeled (31–35 count)

1 pound jumbo lump crabmeat

2–3 teaspoons salt

2 teaspoons fresh ground black pepper

2 teaspoons hot sauce

1 cup chopped parsley

Heat the oil in a large, heavy-duty sauté pan or skillet over medium-high heat. Using a wooden spoon, blend flour into the heated oil and lower the heat. Continue stirring for 8–10 minutes until a dark roux begins to form. Add the andouille, onions, celery, and peppers and cook 5 minutes, stirring often. While this is cooking, strain the fish stock and discard the bones and vegetables. Place 2 quarts of fish stock in a large stock pot and place on a medium heat.

Add the garlic, basil, and thyme to the roux mixture and cook for 1 more minute. Briskly, using a large wire whisk, blend the roux mixture into the slowly simmering stock. Continue stirring for 1–2 minutes, making sure that the roux does not stick to the bottom of the pot.

Add the diced tomatoes, tomato sauce, Rotel tomatoes, and bay leaves and simmer for 10 minutes. Stir in the green onions and shrimp and cook for 15 more minutes. Add the crabmeat, salt, pepper, hot sauce, and parsley and serve.

Yield: 8–10 servings

Shrimp Harrison

My son loves shrimp and grits. This is a dish I developed for him with the richest grits recipe known to man. The grits are good for breakfast, but you might want to invite a cardiologist to join you.

2 pounds (21–25) shrimp, peeled and deveined
1 teaspoon kosher salt
1 teaspoon Old Bay Seasoning
½ teaspoon black pepper, freshly ground
3 tablespoons olive oil
2 cups mushrooms, sliced
1½ teaspoons garlic, minced
½ cup white wine
1 tablespoon white vinegar
¼ cup chicken broth
¾ cup unsalted butter, cut into small cubes
1 cup Caramelized Onions (recipe follows)
2 tablespoons fresh parsley, chopped
1 recipe Really Rich Grits (recipe follows)

Season the shrimp with the salt, Old Bay Seasoning, and black pepper. Place olive oil in a large, heavy-duty sauté pan over high heat. Heat the oil until it just begins to smoke. Carefully place the shrimp in the smoking hot pan. Allow the shrimp to cook without moving them for 2–3 minutes. Add the mushrooms and garlic and cook 5 minutes. Using a slotted spoon, remove the shrimp and hold in a warm place.

Add the white wine and vinegar and reduce until almost no liquid remains. Add the chicken broth and cook until only 1 tablespoon remains. Add the butter cubes and stir constantly until butter has dissolved, being careful not to cook too long (if you cook it too long at this stage, the butter will separate).

Add the caramelized onions and warm shrimp into the pan and stir so that the sauce coats the shrimp. Remove from heat and stir in parsley.

Place ¾ cup of cooked grits into each serving dish, top the grits with the shrimp, and serve immediately.

Yield: 8–10 servings

CARAMELIZED ONIONS

2 tablespoons unsalted butter
3 cups yellow onion, thinly sliced
1 teaspoon kosher salt

Melt butter over medium-low heat in a large sauté pan. Add onions and salt to the melted butter. Cook onions for 15–20 minutes, stirring them often to prevent burning. The onions should continue cooking until a rich brown color is obtained.

REALLY RICH GRITS

1 quart heavy whipping cream
1 cup grits
2 teaspoons salt
1 teaspoon black pepper
1 bay leaf
½ cup unsalted butter, cut into cubes
1 cup Parmesan cheese, grated

Preheat oven to 275°.
    Stir together the cream, grits, salt, pepper, and bay leaf.
Place the mixture in an ovenproof baking dish and cover. Bake for 2¼–3 hours, stirring every 30 minutes.
    Once the grits are soft and creamy, stir in the butter cubes and Parmesan cheese. Serve immediately.

Line-Dried
Mother knows best. Designers gave us leopard print satin sheets but what works best are plain white linens, crisply dried in the sun.

Black Strap Molasses Muffins

This recipe is one of the most requested recipes at the Purple Parrot Café. Don't overmix the batter or the muffins will be tough and dense. They are best when the batter is made at least 8 hours in advance. For a muffin with a completely different flavor profile use honey instead of molasses.

¾ cup hot water
½ cup molasses
¼ cup milk
2 cups whole-wheat flour
2 cups all-purpose flour
3 tablespoons baking soda
1½ tablespoons salt
1½ cups pecans, roasted, cooled
¾ cup sugar

Combine the molasses with the hot water and stir well. Add milk to the molasses mixture and set aside. Sift together the 2 flours, baking soda, and salt. Add nuts and sugar to the sifted flours. Gently fold in the wet ingredients into the flour/nut mixture. Do not overmix (it is fine if there are small clumps of dry mixture still visible). Store batter in refrigerator until ready to bake.

Preheat oven to 325°.

Using a nonstick muffin pan, fill each muffin mold with ⅓ cup of the batter. Bake 15–18 minutes or until an inserted toothpick comes out dry. Let muffins cool slightly before removing them from the muffin pan. Serve warm.

Yield: 12–16 muffins

Raspberry White Chocolate Bread Pudding

A variation on one of our restaurant's most popular desserts. Your guests will love you for making it. Make an extra batch and send them home with a doggie bag.

5 ounces white chocolate

4 egg yolks

1 egg

¾ cup sugar

2 teaspoons vanilla extract

1½ cups heavy whipping cream

½ cup milk

¼ teaspoon salt

1 large loaf of sourdough bread (crusts cut off) cut into 1-inch cubes, approximately
   5 cups of cubes

2 cups frozen raspberries, thawed (reserve juice)

Preheat oven to 350°.

Melt white chocolate in a double boiler.

In another double boiler over moderate heat, combine eggs, sugar, vanilla, whipping cream, milk, and salt and stir well to prevent eggs from scrambling. When the cream mixture is warm, add melted chocolate and stir well.

Fold bread cubes into custard mixture. Let it sit for 5 minutes and then mix on low speed in an electric mixer using the paddle attachment (or mix with your hands, squishing the bread mixture between your fingers until it is completely incorporated and all of the bread has been broken up—wear rubber gloves if the mixture is too hot). Remove the paddle attachment and, using a rubber spatula, gently fold the thawed raspberries into the bread pudding mixture.

Pour into a buttered 2.2-quart Pyrex baking dish and cover with parchment paper. Place the baking dish in a large roasting pan and fill the pan with 2 inches of hot water. Bake for 45 minutes. Remove paper and cook an additional 15 minutes to brown the top.

Raspberry White Chocolate Bread Pudding can be held in the refrigerator for 2 or 3 days. When cooled completely, scoop out individual portions (or use a cookie cutter for unique and interesting shapes—hearts for Valentine's Day, etc) and heat to just warm in a microwave. Top with the warmed sauce.

RASPBERRY WHITE CHOCOLATE SAUCE

8 ounces white chocolate
¼ cup heavy whipping cream, warmed
2 tablespoons raspberry juice
2 tablespoons Framboise liquor

Melt white chocolate in a double boiler. Add heavy cream, raspberry juice, and Framboise and blend thoroughly. This sauce will hold in the refrigerator and can be reheated in the microwave until just warm.

Yield: 8–12 servings

In the Cool of the Awning

Before we had air conditioning, my dad got an ice-laden TV tray, put it in front of a box fan in the window and turned the fan on. We all sat in chairs across from it and got wet. Then my mother sent my father to the Western Auto for a window unit. We stayed in that room a lot that summer.

Southern Summer Supper

Rosemary Roasted Chicken

Fried Corn

Roasted Garlic New Potatoes

21st-Century Turnip Greens

Zucchini-Squash Casserole

Pink-Eyed Purple-Hull Peas

Cornbread

Blueberry-Peach Shortcake
with Vanilla-Bean Custard Ice Cream

Chair and Chair Alike
Adirondack chairs are the perfect outdoor furniture. The armrest doubles as a small table for refreshing beverages from mint juleps to small bottled cokes.

Rosemary Roasted Chicken

Chef Linda Nance created a unique way to spruce up the average roasted chicken. Make this recipe and you'll never buy the premade grocery store variety again.

1 whole chicken, about 4–5 pounds
1 tablespoon bacon fat
1 tablespoon unsalted butter, softened
2 teaspoons kosher salt
2 teaspoons black pepper, freshly ground
2 teaspoons Poultry Seasoning (recipe page 111)
1 small yellow onion, peeled and cut into 8 wedges
1 small ripe orange, cut into 8 wedges
¼ cup celery, small dice
2 tablespoons brown sugar
8 fresh rosemary sprigs

Preheat oven to 350°.

Rinse and dry the chicken. Combine the bacon fat and butter and rub this mixture over the entire chicken. Sprinkle salt, pepper, and poultry seasoning over the entire chicken, including the inside cavity.

Mix together the onion, orange, celery, and brown sugar. Remove the leaves from 2 stems of the rosemary and combine it with the onion mixture. Stuff this mixture into the cavity of the chicken. Use a small paring knife to cut 1 slit at both ends of each breast and 1 slit in each leg and thigh section of the chicken. Gently insert the remaining rosemary springs into the slits.

Truss the chicken and place it on a rack in a roasting pan. Place in the center of the oven. Roast the chicken 45 minutes–1 hour; the thigh juices will run clear when the chicken is done. About 15–20 minutes into the roasting of the chicken, baste the skin with the pan drippings.

Allow the chicken to rest for 10 minutes. Gently remove the inserted rosemary sprigs before carving and serving.

Yield: 4–6 servings

Fried Corn

A Southern supper classic that is best made in June when the sweet corn is available. If you make extra and freeze in one-quart Baggies, your winters can taste like summer with one touch of the defrost button.

8 ears fresh corn
1 tablespoon bacon fat
2 tablespoons unsalted butter
1 teaspoon salt
½ teaspoon black pepper
1 tablespoon sugar

Remove the husks and corn silk from the fresh ears of corn. Using a very sharp knife, cut the corn kernels from the cob. With the back side of the knife, scrape the cobs to remove the remaining pulp and juice.

Melt the bacon fat and butter in a medium-sized heavy skillet or sauté pan over medium heat. Place the corn kernels, pulp, and juice in the skillet. Lower the heat and cook for 15 minutes, stirring often. Sprinkle the cooked corn with salt, pepper, and sugar and serve.

Yield: 8 servings

Roasted Garlic New Potatoes

The smaller the potato, the better. They should be smaller than a golf ball and slightly larger than a jawbreaker.

2½ pounds new red potatoes, small
3 quarts chicken broth (low-sodium if store-bought)
1 stick butter
¼ cup roasted garlic puree
1 teaspoon salt
1 teaspoon black pepper, freshly ground
⅓ cup fresh parsley, chopped

Wash the potatoes thoroughly. Using a paring knife, cut a strip around the outside of the potato. Place potatoes in a large stockpot. Add chicken broth and bring to a boil. Reduce heat and cook at a low simmer 20–30 minutes, until potatoes are fork tender. Drain potatoes. Place hot potatoes in a large skillet with all of the remaining ingredients except the parsley. Simmer over medium heat, stirring gently. Cook 10–12 minutes. Sprinkle with fresh parsley and serve.

Yield: 8 servings

21st-Century Turnip Greens

I cooked a version of this recipe with Chef Marvin Woods on his television show **Home Plate.** You will think there are too many greens for the skillet—don't worry, they cook down quickly. With this recipe you won't need a vinegar-based pepper sauce to sprinkle over the greens when served. The quality of the smoked bacon will make a huge difference in the outcome.

½ cup bacon, medium dice
¼ cup shallots, small dice
¼ cup balsamic vinegar
1 tablespoon brown sugar
½ teaspoon crushed red pepper
2–3 bunches turnip greens, thoroughly cleaned, dried, and cut into 2-inch-wide strips
   (about 10 cups cut up)
1½ cups Pork Stock (recipe page 21)
½ teaspoon kosher salt

In a large saucepan, brown the bacon over medium heat. Stir in the shallots and cook for 2 minutes. Add the vinegar, brown sugar, and crushed red pepper. Cook until the sugar has dissolved completely. Add in the turnip greens and mix them well with the bacon mixture. Add the hot Pork Stock and cover for 5 minutes. Remove the cover and stir the greens. Continue cooking for 10 minutes, stirring often to prevent the greens from burning. Add the salt. Hold warm until ready to serve.

   Yield: 6–8 servings

Zucchini-Squash Casserole

Add shrimp, crabmeat, or crawfish for an interesting lunch entrée.

2 tablespoons olive oil

1½ pounds yellow squash, cut into 1½-inch cubes

1½ pounds zucchini, cut into 1½-inch cubes

1½ teaspoon salt, divided

2 teaspoons Creole Seasoning (recipe page 21)

2 tablespoons unsalted butter

½ cup yellow onion, small dice

¼ cup red bell pepper, small dice

¼ cup celery, small dice

2 teaspoons fresh garlic, minced

1 teaspoon black pepper

¼ cup green onions, sliced thinly

1 tablespoon fresh basil, chopped

½ cup sour cream

¾ cup smoked cheddar or provolone cheese, shredded

1 cup coarse unseasoned bread crumbs

½ cup Parmesan cheese, grated

¼ cup fresh parsley, chopped

2 tablespoons melted butter

Preheat oven to 400°.

In a large mixing bowl, toss the olive oil, squash, 1 teaspoon of salt, and Creole Seasoning. Spread the squash in a large baking pan and roast in the oven for 15 minutes. Remove the squash from the oven and drain in a colander. Gently press against the squash to remove as much excess moisture as possible.

While the squash is roasting, melt butter over medium heat in a small sauté pan. Add the yellow onion, red bell pepper, and celery and cook 2–3 minutes. Add garlic, the remainder of the salt, pepper, and green onions and cook for 3 minutes more.

Place the cooked squash, onion mixture, fresh basil, sour cream, and cheddar cheese in a large mixing bowl. Use a rubber spatula or wooden spoon to gently fold the mixture together until the sour cream is well incorporated.

Lower the oven to 325°.

Place squash mixture into a 2-quart baking dish. Combine the bread crumbs, Parmesan cheese, parsley, and melted butter and top the casserole evenly. Bake 20 minutes.

Yield: 8–10 servings

A Pitcher Is Worth a Thousand Words

Boiling water to make iced tea is one of the great mysteries of life. Sweet tea was developed in the South using green tea. Supplies were cut off during WWII and English colonies like India supplied black tea. Now with Americans becoming more health conscious, some are returning to the original recipe.

Pink-Eyed Purple-Hull Peas

These are best when made a day ahead of time. Keep pork stock in your freezer and use when cooking all manner of peas, beans, and greens.

3 cups fresh peas—black-eyed, crowder, lady, or pink-eyed purple-hull
4 cups Pork Stock (recipe follows)
1 strip bacon
2 teaspoons sugar
2 teaspoons salt
1 tablespoon flour

Place peas, stock, bacon, sugar, and salt in a 2-quart saucepan over medium heat. Bring to a boil. Reduce heat to a slow simmer and cover. Simmer 30–45 minutes. Remove ¼ cup of pot liquor. Stir flour into pot liquor and pour back into peas. Bring back to a simmer and cook 10 minutes more. Remove from heat and let rest for 10 minutes before serving.

Yield: 6–8 servings

PORK STOCK

8 ham hocks
1½ gallon water
½ onion

Place hocks, water, and onion in a large stockpot and simmer over low heat 8 hours. Add more water as needed to yield 1 gallon of final product. Strain and place stock in refrigerator overnight. Using a large spoon, remove fat layer from top of chilled stock. Stock should be slightly gelatinous. Stock can be frozen in small batches.

Yield: 1 gallon

Note: Reserve ham hock meat for other recipes

Cornbread

If you want to start a fight at the dinner table, bring up the sugar-or-no-sugar–in-your-cornbread argument. Deciding which version is best—Southern or Yankee—can be a more controversial topic than religion or politics.

1 cup all-purpose flour, unbleached
1 cup self-rising cornmeal
6 tablespoons sugar
1 teaspoon baking powder
½ teaspoon salt
1 cup half-and-half
⅓ cup butter, melted (or oil)
1 egg, large and slightly beaten

Preheat oven to 400°.

Grease an 8 x 8-inch baking pan or cast-iron skillet with vegetable shortening, bacon grease, or nonstick cooking spray. Sift flour, cornmeal, sugar, baking powder, and salt into a mixing bowl. Form a well in the mixture and add half-and-half, butter, and egg. Stir until just combined. Do not overwork batter. Bake to golden brown or until a toothpick inserted in the center comes out clean (approximately 12–15 minutes depending on oven).

Yield: 6–8 slices

Blueberry-Peach Shortcake with Vanilla-Bean Custard Ice Cream

The shortcake dough can be made and frozen in advance. Homemade peach ice cream works well, too.

2 cups all-purpose flour
1 tablespoon baking powder
⅛ teaspoon salt
2 tablespoons sugar + extra for sprinkling
¾ cup cold unsalted butter (1½ sticks), diced
3 large eggs, lightly beaten
¼ cup heavy cream, chilled
¼ cup sour cream
1 teaspoon vanilla extract
1 egg beaten with 2 tablespoons water or milk, for egg wash
¼ cup sugar
4–5 ripe peaches, peeled, pitted, and thinly sliced (about 3 cups)
1 tablespoon fresh lemon juice
Vanilla Bean Custard Ice Cream (recipe follows)
1 pint blueberries

Preheat the oven to 400°.

Sift the flour, baking powder, salt, and 2 tablespoons of sugar into the bowl of an electric mixer fitted with the paddle attachment. Blend in the butter at the lowest speed and mix until the mixture is the size of peas. Combine the eggs, heavy cream, sour cream, and vanilla extract and quickly add to the flour and butter mixture. Mix until just blended. The dough will be sticky.

Dump the dough out onto a well-floured surface. Flour your hands and pat the dough out ¾-inch thick. You should see lumps of butter in the dough.

Cut shortcakes with a 2¾-inch cutter and place on a baking sheet lined with parchment. Brush the tops with the egg wash. Sprinkle with sugar and bake for 20–25 minutes, until the outsides are crisp and the insides are fully baked. Let cool on a wire rack.

While the shortcakes are baking, combine ¼ cup of sugar with the sliced peaches and lemon juice. Refrigerate until needed.

Split each shortcake in half crosswise and place the bottom half on a plate. Place a small amount of the peach mixture atop each biscuit bottom. Place 1 scoop of ice cream

Southern Bell

The Southeast is an agricultural society. In olden days when workers were doing chores in the fields, the dinner bell was the signal to come eat.

on the peaches and spoon the remaining peach mixture over the ice cream. Place the shortcake top over the filled bottom half and sprinkle each one with 2–3 tablespoons of fresh blueberries. Serve immediately.

Yield: 6–8 servings

VANILLA-BEAN CUSTARD ICE CREAM

5 cups heavy cream
2½ cups whole milk
pinch salt
1½ cups sugar
1 vanilla bean
12 large egg yolks

Combine the cream, milk, salt, and ¾ cup of the sugar in a large pot. Split the vanilla bean down the middle lengthwise and scrape out the seeds with a paring knife; add them to the pot and toss in the pods for added flavor. Place the cream mixture over medium heat and bring to a simmer, stirring with a wooden spoon to dissolve the sugar. Cook for about 15 minutes, being careful that the mixture does not boil, simmer, or scald. Shut off the heat, cover the pot, and allow the cream mixture to steep for 15 minutes to further infuse the vanilla flavor.

In the meantime, lightly blend the egg yolks in a large mixing bowl with a wire whisk. Gradually add the remaining ¾ cup of sugar and continue to whisk until the sugar is completely dissolved and the eggs are thick and pale yellow (approximately 6 minutes). Using a large ladle or measuring cup, temper the eggs by gradually whisking in about 2 cups of the hot cream mixture. Return this back to the rest of the cream in the saucepan and turn the heat to medium-low. Stir constantly until the custard thickens and leaves a path on the back of a spoon when you run your finger across it, about 10–12 minutes (do not let it boil).

Pour the vanilla custard through a fine strainer into a mixing bowl and place it over an ice bath and chill completely. Stir the mixture while it is cooling. For best flavor results, store the ice cream base covered overnight in the refrigerator.

Following the manufacturer's instructions of your ice cream freezer, prepare the ice cream. Transfer to airtight containers and freeze until needed.

Yield: ½ gallon

Dinner on the Grounds

Buttermilk Fried Chicken

Ham with a Twist

Green Bean Casserole

Deviled Eggs x 3

Blackberry-Raspberry Cobbler

Yeast Rolls with Honey Butter

Peach Ice Cream

Buttermilk Fried Chicken

Marinating in the buttermilk overnight is the key to plump, juicy fried chicken. Smaller chicken pieces work best.

1 tablespoon Poultry Seasoning (recipe follows)
2 cups buttermilk
2 whole chickens (2–3 pounds each), cleaned and cut into 8 pieces
2 cups white flour
1 tablespoon kosher salt
1 tablespoon black pepper, freshly ground

Combine the poultry seasoning and buttermilk. Submerge the cut chicken in the buttermilk. Cover tightly and refrigerate for at least 12 hours.

Fill an electric skillet approximately 1-inch with fryer shortening and set at 350°.

Blend the flour, salt, and pepper. Coat the chicken in the flour mixture and fry for 20–30 minutes (10–15 minutes on each side). Longer for the thighs, shorter for the wings. Let rest for 10 minutes after frying.

Yield 6–8 servings

POULTRY SEASONING

¼ cup Lawry's Seasoned Salt
¼ cup garlic powder
¼ cup white pepper
¼ cup lemon pepper
¼ cup celery salt

Combine and mix well. Store in an airtight container.

With Heads Bowed

When sunflowers are heavy with seeds they turn their heads to the ground. During long prayers in church the rest of us just look at our shoes.

Ham with a Twist

Try this with Dr Pepper or root beer. The finished product is beautiful. It's also great for holiday gift giving.

GLAZE

2 12-ounce bottles Orange Crush
¼ cup orange juice, freshly squeezed
2 tablespoons mayhaw or muscadine jelly
2 bay leaves
2 tablespoons Pickapeppa Sauce
1 teaspoon garlic, minced
2 tablespoons shallots, minced
5 cloves
1 cinnamon stick
1 tablespoon orange zest, freshly grated
2 teaspoons lemon zest, freshly grated
2 teaspoons lime zest, freshly grated

Preheat oven to 350°.

Combine all ingredients for the glaze in a small saucepan. Place over medium heat and simmer for 30 minutes. Strain the liquid and discard the solids. Return the mixture to the stove and reduce until approximately ¾ cup liquid remains.

HAM

1 cured smoked ham, 10–12 pounds
1 teaspoon dry mustard
1 cup light brown sugar

Place ham on a V-shaped roasting rack in a disposable roasting pan (or a roasting pan lined with foil). Using a paring knife, cut shallow slits in a crisscross pattern on the top of the ham. Spoon 2 tablespoons of the glaze over the top of the ham. Combine dry mustard and brown sugar and press the mixture over the entire surface of the ham. Pour 1 cup of water into the bottom of the roasting pan and place the ham on the V-shaped roasting rack, then into the oven.

Spoon 1–2 tablespoons of the glaze over the ham every 15–20 minutes until you have used the entire batch of glaze. Try to get the glaze on as much of the outer surface of the ham as possible.

Bake the ham to an internal temperature of 160°. Remove from oven and allow to rest 30 minutes before carving.

Yield: 10–14 servings

Green Bean Casserole

Not your typical green bean casserole with fried onions on top. Best when made a day in advance. Let the casserole come to room temperature before baking.

1 quart chicken broth
4 14.5-ounce cans green beans, drained
¼ cup bacon, very small dice
½ cup yellow onion, small dice
¼ cup red bell pepper, small dice
¼ cup green bell pepper, small dice
2 teaspoons garlic, minced
1 teaspoon Creole Seasoning (recipe page 21)
1 teaspoon black pepper
1 cup sour cream
½ cup sharp cheddar, shredded
1 cup Panko bread crumbs
⅓ cup Parmesan cheese, grated
¼ cup fresh parsley, chopped
2 tablespoons melted butter

Preheat oven to 350°.

In a large saucepan, bring chicken broth to a boil. Place green beans in the broth and gently simmer 10 minutes. Drain the green beans.

Place the bacon in a medium sauté pan and cook it until it become brown and crispy, stirring often to prevent burning. Add the onion and peppers and sauté over medium-high heat for 3 minutes. Add garlic, Creole Seasoning, and black pepper and cook an additional 3 minutes.

Gently combine green beans, sautéed bacon/vegetable mixture, sour cream, and cheddar in a large stainless steel bowl. Place in a 2-quart baking dish. Cover the dish with foil and bake for 20 minutes.

Combine the bread crumbs, Parmesan cheese, parsley, and melted butter. Remove the foil and top with the bread crumb mixture. Bake for 10–15 more minutes, until the topping is light brown in color. Let casserole sit for 10 minutes before serving.

Yield: 8 servings

Deviled Eggs *x 3*

Make double the amount and use the leftovers to make a bold and unique egg salad. This works for each of the three recipes.

For the Hard-boiled Eggs:
Place 24 eggs in a large pot. Add cool water, enough to cover the eggs by 2 inches. Add 1 tablespoon of salt to the water. Place the pot on high heat and cook for 20 minutes. Drain the water from the eggs and cover completely with ice water. Peel eggs once they are cool enough to handle. Store covered and refrigerated if eggs are not going to be used immediately.

SMOKEY BACON AND CHEDDAR DEVILED EGGS

8 large hard-cooked eggs, peeled
⅓ cup mayonnaise
1 teaspoon yellow mustard
¼ teaspoon salt
¼ teaspoon black pepper, freshly ground
1 tablespoon fresh chives, sliced very thin, divided
3 strips bacon, good quality, cooked until crisp and chopped fine
2 tablespoons sharp cheddar cheese, finely shredded

Halve the eggs lengthwise. Gently remove the yolks and place in a small mixing bowl. Reserve the whites.

Using a fork, smash the yolks together with the mayonnaise, yellow mustard, salt, black pepper, and half of the chives. Once the mixture is smooth, fold in the bacon and cheese. Fill each half of the egg whites with the yolk mixture and garnish each one with the remaining chives. Cover and refrigerate until ready to serve.

Yield: 16 pieces

CREOLE CRABMEAT DEVILED EGGS

8 large hard-cooked eggs, peeled
2 tablespoons mayonnaise
2 teaspoons Creole mustard
1 tablespoon lemon juice, freshly squeezed
⅛ teaspoon Creole Seasoning (recipe page 21)
¼ teaspoon hot sauce
1 tablespoon pimiento, very finely chopped and patted dry
2 teaspoons red onion, very finely minced

Ant Bites
When the weather is good, eating outdoors can be sweet. But be careful how the sweets attract black ants. In modern history, fire ants have been introduced from Brazil making the challenge even greater.

⅓ pound lump crabmeat, picked thoroughly to remove shells and cartilage
2 teaspoons fresh parsley, chopped

Halve the eggs lengthwise. Gently remove yolks and place in a small mixing bowl. Reserve the whites.

Using a fork, smash yolks together with the mayonnaise, Creole mustard, lemon juice, Creole Seasoning, and hot sauce. Once the yolk mixture is smooth, fold in the pimiento, red onion, and crabmeat. Fill each half of the egg whites with the yolk mixture and garnish each one with the chopped parsley. Cover and refrigerate until ready to serve.

Yield: 16 pieces

SPICY DEVILED EGGS

8 large hard-cooked eggs, peeled
1 tablespoon mayonnaise
2 tablespoons sour cream
1 teaspoon Dijon mustard
1 teaspoon horseradish
½ teaspoon dry mustard
1 teaspoon white wine vinegar
⅛ teaspoon cayenne pepper
⅛ teaspoon black pepper, freshly ground
1 teaspoon fresh jalapeño, seeds removed and chopped fine
1 tablespoon dill pickle, chopped fine
1 teaspoon sweet pickle relish
2 tablespoons green onion, very thinly sliced
½ teaspoon Creole Seasoning (recipe page 21)

Halve the eggs lengthwise. Gently remove yolks and place in a small mixing bowl. Reserve the whites.

Using a fork, smash the yolks and mix with mayonnaise, sour cream, Dijon mustard, horseradish, dry mustard, vinegar, cayenne, and black pepper until smooth. Add jalapeño, dill pickle, relish, and green onions. Fill each half of the egg whites with yolk mixture and garnish each with Creole Seasoning. Cover and refrigerate until ready to serve.

Yield: 16 pieces

Blackberry-Raspberry Cobbler

Fresh fruits are best but frozen will work fine. The cream cheese pastry can also be used for pie dough and turnovers.

PASTRY

1 cup butter, softened
1 8-ounce package cream cheese, softened
½ teaspoon salt
2 cups flour

By hand or using a paddle attachment on an electric mixer, combine all ingredients to form a soft dough. Do not overmix. Wrap the dough well and refrigerate 10–12 hours before using.

When ready to use, remove dough from refrigerator and allow to sit at room temperature 10–15 minutes.

FILLING

4 cups blackberries, fresh or frozen (thawed if frozen)
3 cups frozen raspberries, thawed and drained
½ cup sugar
⅓ cup brown sugar
2 teaspoons lemon juice
1 tablespoon orange juice
¾ cup flour
1½ teaspoons cinnamon
1 egg
2 tablespoons milk

Preheat oven to 350°. Lightly butter a 9 x 13-inch baking dish.

Allow the prepared pastry to come to room temperature 1 hour before preparing the cobbler.

Divide dough into half. On a floured surface, roll out half the dough into a 9 x 13-inch rectangle, ¼-inch thick. Place the dough in the baking dish and bake 10 minutes. Remove the par-cooked dough from the oven and allow it to cool.

Place the berries in a large mixing bowl and sprinkle with sugar, brown sugar, lemon juice, and orange juice. Gently mix. Combine flour and cinnamon together. Sprinkle the berries with the flour mixture and gently fold in. Spread the berry mixture over the top of the par-baked pastry.

On a floured surface roll out the remaining dough into a 9 x 13-inch rectangle. Using a sharp knife, cut ½-inch-wide strips. Arrange the strips into a lattice design atop the berries.

Whisk together the egg and milk and, using a pastry brush, egg wash the dough. Place the prepared cobbler on a sheet pan and bake for 35–40 minutes. Let the cobbler cool 20 minutes before serving.

Yield: Feeds 12–14 people

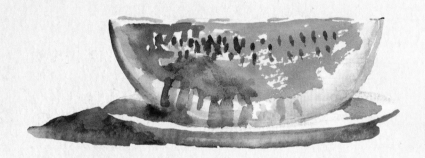

When Life Gives You Lemons
All big business begins with small business. This partnership between brother and sister is a competitive collaboration. The Chamber of Commerce should have a place for these guys.

Yeast Rolls with Honey Butter

A staple from the school cafeterias of my youth. The dough can be frozen after the rolls have been formed. Honey Butter should always be in your fridge.

1 package active dry yeast
¼ cup warm water
¾ cup milk, scalded
¼ cup sugar
1½ teaspoons salt
1 egg + 1 egg yolk, beaten
4 cups all-purpose flour, divided
¼ cup unsalted butter, softened

Dissolve the yeast in warm water. Blend the hot milk, sugar, and salt in a mixing bowl. Allow mixture to cool to lukewarm. Beat in the egg and egg yolk. Stir the dissolved yeast into the milk mixture.

Place 2 cups of the flour and the soft butter in a mixing bowl and using the dough hook attachment on an electric mixer, blend the butter with the flour. Add the milk mixture and knead until smooth. Gradually add in more flour and knead until the dough leaves the sides of the bowl. Continue to knead, for 8–10 minutes, until the dough is smooth and elastic.

Place the dough in a large buttered mixing bowl and turn it once or twice to butter the entire surface. Cover with a slightly damp cloth and place in a warm place. Allow dough to rise until doubled in size. Press the dough down into the bowl to remove air bubbles.

Put a little butter or shortening on your hands and divide the dough into small pieces, about 2 ounces in size. Roll into balls and place on a shallow greased baking pan with the sides touching. (If you want to freeze the rolls, do so here.) Cover loosely with a cloth and place the rolls in a warm place. Allow rolls to rise until doubled in size.

Preheat oven to 400°. Bake 12–15 minutes.

Yield: 18–24 rolls

HONEY BUTTER

1 cup unsalted butter, softened
⅓ cup honey
1 teaspoon lemon juice
½ teaspoon kosher salt

Using an electric mixer, beat butter until light and fluffy. Add in the remaining ingredients and blend well. Refrigerate until needed, but allow the Honey Butter to come to room temperature before serving.

Peach Ice Cream

Nothing tastes like summer more than peach ice cream. The custard is an extra step but well worth the effort.

2 cups fresh peaches, peeled and cut into ½-inch pieces (frozen peaches can be substituted)
¾ cups sugar, divided
1 tablespoon lemon juice, freshly squeezed
2 tablespoons peach schnapps
1 cup heavy cream
½ cup milk
½ vanilla bean
2 egg yolks

In a bowl, combine peaches, ¼ cup sugar, lemon juice, and peach schnapps. Cover and refrigerate 2–3 hours, stirring occasionally.

Remove peach mixture from refrigerator, drain, and reserve the juice. Return peaches to refrigerator.

In a medium saucepan, combine remaining sugar, heavy cream, milk, and the vanilla bean, split in half lengthwise. Heat just until just boiling.

In a separate bowl, vigorously whisk egg yolks. While whisking, slowly add ⅓ of the boiled cream mixture. Stir well. Add remaining egg mixture to cream mixture. Return to low-medium heat and continue stirring for 5–7 minutes. Just as it begins to simmer, remove from heat and strain into a bowl set over ice. Add the reserved peach juice. Stir well until completely chilled.

Transfer the mixture to an ice cream maker and freeze according to manufacturer's instructions. After the ice cream begins to stiffen, add the peaches and continue to freeze until done. Remove the ice cream from the ice cream maker and store in an airtight container in the freezer until ready to serve.

Yield: 8 servings

**To Everything
Churn, Churn, Churn**

I would start cranking the ice cream churn, but when my arm began to tire I would sit on some newspapers on top and my older brother, Jim, would turn. When he could turn no more, we knew it was done.

A Tale of Two Tailgates

Chilled Yellowfin Tuna with Mojo Mustard
and Wasabi Cream

Boiled Shrimp with Seafood Remoulade Sauce
and Cocktail Sauce

Miniature Smoked Tenderloin Sandwiches
with Three Spreads

Broiled and Chilled Asparagus
with Dill Mayonnaise

Pesto Potato Salad

Artichoke and Crab Dip

BBQ Ribs

Caramel Brownies

Caddy Corner
The SEC didn't invent the phenomenon but down South tailgating has become an art form. This Cadillac trunk becomes a fine dining restaurant before a football game.

PAGES 124–125:
Four and Twenty Blackbirds
I am not sure how birds migrate the way they do. If you don't believe in God you have to believe in something when you see an endless stream of birds across the sky. They look like a wave of birds.

Chilled Yellowfin Tuna with Mojo Mustard and Wasabi Cream

Fresh yellowfin tuna is a must. Purchase the best quality you can find. It must be seared rare. Make sure you are using a super-sharp knife when cutting thin slices of tuna. When drizzling the sauces, do not cover the bright red tuna completely. The presentation is best when the bright red is visible. Instead of sesame crackers, substitute wonton wrappers, deep-fried until crisp, drained, and cooled.

1–2 tablespoons sesame oil
1½ pounds fresh yellowfin tuna, preferably 1 large elongated piece the size of a rolling pin
1 tablespoon kosher salt
½ tablespoon black pepper, freshly ground

In a large sauté pan, heat the sesame oil until smoking. Season the tuna with the salt and pepper, and sear each side in the hot oil. You should cook the tuna just long enough to achieve a subtle red brown color on each side. The tuna should not be cooked to more than medium-rare. Cool the tuna immediately and prepare the sauces.

MOJO MUSTARD

⅓ cup sweet chili pepper sauce for chicken(found in oriental markets)
⅓ cup Dijon mustard
1 teaspoon ginger, minced
2 teaspoons soy sauce

Mix together all ingredients and chill before serving.

WASABI CREAM

2 tablespoons dry wasabi powder
3 tablespoons hot water
⅓ cup sour cream
2 teaspoons lime juice, freshly squeezed
½ teaspoon salt

In a small mixing bowl, blend together the wasabi powder and hot water to form a thick paste. Add in the remaining ingredients and blend well.

Using a very sharp knife, cut very thin cross-section pieces of the tuna (¼-inch discs cutting against the grain). Arrange the sliced tuna on a serving platter (as you would spread a deck of cards) and drizzle with the 2 sauces. Serve with a high-quality sesame cracker

Yield: 10–12 appetizer servings

Boiled Shrimp with Seafood Remoulade Sauce and Cocktail Sauce

Spreading the shrimp on cookie sheets helps them to cool much faster. Most foods continue to cook a little while even though removed from the heat. To make shrimp last longer at a party, don't peel them. If the peeling is left for the guests to do, only the hard-core shrimp eaters will last the duration (include me in that number). Remoulade sauce tastes better if made at least 1 day in advance.

3 quarts water
5 tablespoons salt
2 tablespoons liquid crab boil
2 bay leaves
½ cup white wine
1 lemon, halved
5 pounds large shrimp, shell on

Place everything except the shrimp in an 8-quart stockpot. Bring the mixture to a simmer and cook for 5 minutes. Add the shrimp and cook for 5–7 minutes. Drain and spread the shrimp onto cookie sheets. Refrigerate immediately to stop the cooking process.
   Yield: 8–10 servings

SEAFOOD REMOULADE SAUCE

¼ cup celery, finely chopped
⅓ cup onion, finely chopped
½ cup ketchup
1 teaspoon Creole mustard
1½ tablespoon lemon juice, freshly squeezed
1 tablespoon prepared horseradish
½ cup mayonnaise
½ teaspoon Creole Seasoning (recipe page 21)
½ teaspoon Lawry's Seasoned Salt
½ teaspoon garlic, minced

Place onion and celery into a mixing bowl. Add remaining ingredients and blend well.

Yield: 2 cups

COCKTAIL SAUCE

1½ cups ketchup
3 tablespoons freshly squeezed lemon juice
2 teaspoons Worcestershire sauce
¼ cup prepared horseradish
½ teaspoon black pepper, freshly ground
1½ teaspoons salt

Combine all ingredients and mix well. Refrigerate 2 hours before serving.

Yield: 2 cups

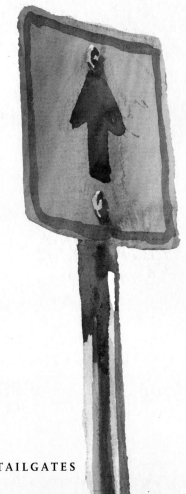

Miniature Smoked Tenderloin Sandwiches with Three Spreads

All of the spreads have a great shelf life. The Honey-Spiked Creole Mustard is good with chicken or pork. It can be added to a chicken-salad recipe to supplement the typical mayonnaise addition. Chutney is in the pickle section of your local market. This is a good sauce to serve with grilled chicken. The quality of the roll that you serve with the tenderloin can make or break the sandwiches.

5–6 cups wood chips
2-pound beef tenderloin, trimmed and cleaned
2 tablespoons bacon grease, melted
1 tablespoon steak seasoning
½ teaspoon black pepper, freshly ground
24 dinner rolls, varied styles and flavors, cut in half crosswise

Soak wood chips for 2–3 hours and drain well. Prepare grill or smoker to cook at 275°.

Rub tenderloin with melted bacon grease and sprinkle with steak seasoning and pepper. Cook tenderloin 45–50 minutes, to an internal temperature of 130°. Add more chips as needed to keep the smoke flowing. Remove from heat and let tenderloin cool completely.

Slice ¼-inch-thin slices of the beef tenderloin and arrange on a serving tray. Serve the cut rolls and 3 sauces on the side and allow guests to build their own sandwiches.

All of the sauces may be made 3–4 days in advance and stored in the refrigerator until needed.

Yield: 24 sandwiches

HORSERADISH SPREAD

¼ cup sour cream
½ cup mayonnaise
¼ teaspoon black pepper, freshly ground
3 tablespoons prepared horseradish
2 tablespoons red onion, minced
¼ teaspoon garlic, minced

The Ride Home
When the school buses lined up, we were all excited about being out for the day. They were called Bluebirds but were as yellow as Orioles. Sometimes on Friday afternoons I would ride home to a friend's. You think it will always be that easy to make good friends, but it's not.

1 tablespoon chives, chopped
1 tablespoon parsley, chopped
½ teaspoon salt

Combine all ingredients in a mixing bowl and store covered and refrigerated until ready to serve.

CHUTNEY MAYO

1 tablespoon olive oil
2 tablespoons yellow onion, minced
2 teaspoons garlic, minced
¼ teaspoon salt
½ teaspoon curry powder
2 tablespoons sherry
¾ cup mango chutney
¾ cup mayonnaise

In a small sauté pan, heat olive oil over low heat. Place onion, garlic, salt, and curry powder in the hot oil and cook 1 minute. Add the sherry and reduce. Remove from heat and cool completely. Once the cooked mixture is cooled, combine it with the remaining ingredients. Store covered and refrigerated until ready to serve.

HONEY-SPIKED CREOLE MUSTARD

½ cup Creole mustard
1 tablespoon yellow mustard
2 tablespoon sour cream
1 tablespoon mayonnaise
¼ cup honey
1 teaspoon prepared horseradish
2 teaspoons fresh parsley, chopped
1 teaspoon fresh thyme leaves, chopped
⅛ teaspoon cayenne pepper
½ teaspoon lemon juice
¼ teaspoon salt

Using a wire whisk, combine all ingredients. Store covered and refrigerated until ready to serve.

Broiled and Chilled Asparagus with Dill Mayonnaise

Always use fresh herbs, but if you must use dried, reduce the amount by half. The asparagus should be medium-sized. Too small and they will be too hard to pick up. The mayonnaise may be held refrigerated for 1 week.

ASPARAGUS

2 pounds fresh asparagus
3 tablespoons olive oil
2 teaspoons kosher salt
1 teaspoon black pepper, freshly ground

Preheat oven to broil.

Toss the asparagus with olive oil, salt, and pepper. Arrange the asparagus on a sheet pan and broil for 5–6 minutes

Note: Asparagus can be baked in an oven set to "broil." Place on a cookie sheet, roll in olive oil, sprinkle with salt and pepper, and broil for 5 minutes, or until al dente.

DILL MAYONNAISE

2 egg yolks
1 teaspoon salt
½ teaspoon Dijon mustard
1½ teaspoons lemon juice, freshly squeezed
1 cup canola oil
1 teaspoon white vinegar
¼ cup fresh dill, chopped

In a small mixing bowl, whisk together the egg yolks, salt, and mustard. When mixture becomes light in color, add lemon juice. Blend.

Drizzle half of the oil slowly into the yolk mixture, whisking constantly. Stir in vinegar. Continue whisking and add remaining oil. Add fresh dill.

To serve, arrange the chilled asparagus on a serving platter. Serve the mayonnaise on the side for dipping.

Yield: 6–8 servings

Pesto Potato Salad

Better when made a day in advance. Let it sit out 1 hour before eating. Best when eaten at room temperature.

6 cups Idaho potatoes peeled and cut into a large dice (¾-inch square)
3 quarts water
2 teaspoons salt
2 cups mayonnaise
¾ cup fresh pesto
2 tablespoons cider vinegar
1 teaspoon white pepper
2 teaspoons black pepper, freshly ground
2 teaspoons salt
1 cup green onion, chopped
1 cup red bell pepper, small dice
1 cup celery, small dice
4 eggs, hard-boiled and chopped

Place potatoes and salt in water and simmer on low heat until potatoes are tender. Drain and allow to cool.

Make the dressing by combining mayonnaise, pesto, vinegar, peppers, and salt. Blend well.

Place the potatoes, onion, bell pepper, celery, and eggs in a large stainless steel bowl. Gently fold in the dressing and mix well.

Yield: 8–10 servings

Artichoke and Crab Dip

Regulate the heat by adding or subtracting hot sauce. Make sure to fold the crabmeat gently. For a unique entrée toss with a half a pound of spaghetti, place in a casserole and bake at 350° until bubbly.

1 tablespoon olive oil
⅓ cup green onions, chopped
2 teaspoons garlic, minced
1 cup artichoke hearts, drained, rough chopped
1 teaspoon salt
2 teaspoons Creole Seasoning (recipe page 21)
¼ teaspoon black pepper, freshly ground
½ teaspoon cayenne pepper
¾ pound cream cheese, softened
½ sour cream
2 large eggs, beaten
1 tablespoon lemon juice, freshly squeezed
½ cup Parmesan cheese, freshly grated
1 tablespoon hot sauce
1 pound lump crabmeat
butter, as needed

Preheat oven to 350˚.

Place oil in a medium sauté pan. Over medium heat cook green onions 1 minute. Add garlic, artichoke hearts, salt, Creole Seasoning, black pepper, and cayenne to the sauté pan and cook 5 minutes, stirring often to prevent burning. Remove from the heat and allow mixture to cool for 10–15 minutes.

Using the paddle attachment on an electric mixer, beat the cream cheese until light and fluffy. Scrape the sides and bottom of the bowl with a rubber spatula and add the sour cream, eggs, lemon juice, Parmesan cheese, and hot sauce. Blend thoroughly.

Using a rubber spatula, first gently fold the artichoke mixture into the cream cheese mixture, then gently fold in the crabmeat until just blended. Place all in a buttered, 1–quart casserole dish and bake until lightly browned.

Allow to set approximately 30 minutes. Serve warm with crackers.

Yield: 1 quart

BBQ Ribs

This recipe calls for pork ribs, but it tastes great with beef ribs, too. The flavor profile will actually work with all slow-cooked meats such as pork shoulder, brisket, and chicken.

3 full racks pork spareribs (each rack should be 3 pounds or less)
1 cup white vinegar
¼ cup paprika
2 tablespoons garlic powder
1 tablespoon onion powder
2 teaspoons black pepper, freshly ground
1 tablespoon kosher salt
2 tablespoons brown sugar
¼ cup sugar
2 teaspoons Creole Seasoning (recipe page 21)

Place the ribs in a large roasting pan or baking dish and pour vinegar over the ribs. Using your hands, rub ribs with the vinegar, and allow them to marinate 3 hours. Drain the vinegar and dry racks with paper towels.

Combine the paprika, garlic powder, onion powder, black pepper, kosher salt, brown sugar, sugar, and Creole Seasoning, and coat the ribs completely. Cover and refrigerate overnight.

Prepare the charcoal according to the directions on the grill for slow barbecuing. Place the ribs on the grill and cook slowly 3–4 hours. The meat should begin to draw away from the bone at the tip, and the ribs should "bend" when picked up with tongs.

Once the ribs are cooked, remove from the grill and cut into 2–3 bone sections, and serve with BBQ sauce on the side.

Yield: 6–8 servings

Where There's Smoke There's Barbeque

This homemade barbeque smoker, looking as if it could be a cannon towed behind a WWII jeep, needs no advertisement when it begins to cook.

BBQ SAUCE

2 tablespoons bacon grease
¼ cup dehydrated onion
1 tablespoon garlic, minced
¼ cup brown sugar
¼ cup sugar
¼ cup molasses
2 cups chicken stock
1 quart ketchup

1½ tablespoon black pepper, freshly ground

¼ teaspoon cayenne pepper

2 tablespoons dry mustard

2 tablespoons lemon juice

¼ cup Worcestershire sauce

½ cup balsamic vinegar

½ cup cider vinegar

Preheat oven to 300°.

In a 3-quart Dutch oven, heat the bacon grease over low heat. Add the dehydrated onion and garlic and cook 3–4 minutes more. Stir in the remaining ingredients and place the sauce in the oven. Bake 2 hours, stirring every 15 minutes.

Store in an airtight container in the refrigerator.

Yield: 8–10 servings

Caramel Brownies

These are the best brownies I have ever eaten. Be careful when cooking the caramel not to overcook. If you get it too dark, start over. This recipe is great without the caramel, too.

CARAMEL
1 cup sugar
¼ cup water
1¼ cup heavy whipping cream, heated

In a small, heavy-duty saucepan, combine the sugar and water. Bring the mixture to a slow boil, stirring very often. Continue to cook until the mixture reaches a deep caramel color, about 10 minutes. As soon as this deep color is achieved, use a wire whisk and quickly stir in the warm cream. Return the caramel to a medium heat and cook for 2–3 more minutes.

Keep warm while preparing the brownie batter.

BROWNIE MIX

6 ounces unsweetened chocolate
1 cup unsalted butter, cut into small cubes
1 cup all-purpose flour
¼ cup cocoa
1 teaspoon double-acting baking powder
⅛ teaspoon salt
4 large eggs
2½ cups sugar
2 teaspoons vanilla extract
1½ cup pecans, chopped (optional)

Preheat oven to 350°. Butter a 9 x 12-inch baking dish.

In a small, heavy saucepan, melt chocolate and butter over low heat. Stir constantly until the mixture is smooth. Remove from the heat and allow the mixture to cool completely.

Sift together flour, cocoa, baking powder, and salt in a large bowl.

Using the whip attachment of an electric mixer, beat the eggs on medium speed. While still beating, add the sugar, a little at a time, and continue to beat 2–3 minutes, until the mixture becomes thick and pale. Add in the chocolate mixture and vanilla and mix well. Add the flour mixture and blend using a rubber spatula or wooden spoon. Stir in the chopped pecans.

Pour the batter into the prepared baking pan and smooth out the top. Drizzle the caramel in rows lengthwise on top of the batter. Drag a pairing knife back and forth through the caramel lines. Bake the brownies 25–30 minutes, or until the brownies pull away slightly from the sides of the pan and/or a toothpick inserted in the center comes out clean. Let brownies cool completely before cutting.

Yield: 16 brownies

Swing Both Ways
This is the closest you can get to flying without wings. An oak tree displays the two popular approaches to tree swings.

Five–F Family Supper

Chopped Salad

Three-Meat Meatloaf

Buttermilk-Cream Cheese Mashed Potatoes

Creamed Spinach

Corn on the Cob with a Twist

The Ultimate Chocolate Cake

Caramel Ribbon Ice Cream

To Kill a Mockingbird
Ah, the balance of nature. The birds give this cat a hard time, but every cat has his day. I wonder about a person who has this many birdhouses and also loves cats.

Chopped Salad

This recipe was inspired by a longstanding recipe from the Junior League of Jackson, Mississippi. It has been a staple in my family's suppers for years.

DRESSING

½ cup sugar
½ cup brown sugar
2 teaspoons Creole mustard
¼ cup red wine vinegar
¼ cup balsamic vinegar
1 tablespoon soy sauce
1 tablespoon fresh shallot, minced
1 teaspoon salt
1 teaspoon black pepper, freshly ground

Place all ingredients in a mixing bowl and blend thoroughly with a wire whisk. This may be made a day or two in advance and held in the refrigerator.

SALAD

1 head fresh romaine lettuce
¼ cup unsalted butter
½ cup walnuts, chopped
½ package ramen noodles, uncooked and broken into small pieces (discard seasoning packet)
1 cup fresh broccoli cut into very small bits
¼ cup green onions, thinly sliced
½ cup dried apricots, chopped

Use a very sharp knife to cut the romaine into 2-inch pieces. Wash and dry the lettuce very well. Refrigerate covered while preparing the other ingredients.

Place the butter in a medium sauté pan over low-medium heat. Once the butter is melted and begins to bubble slightly, stir in the walnuts and ramen pieces. Cook for 5–6 minutes, stirring constantly to prevent burning. Remove from heat and place the toasted nuts and noodles on a paper towel to drain and cool.

In a large mixing bowl, combine the lettuce, nut mixture, broccoli, green onions, and apricots. Stir the dressing well before drizzling it over the salad. Toss the salad until the lettuce is well coated with dressing and serve immediately.

Yield: 6–8 servings

Three-Meat Meatloaf

This is one of the best meatloaf recipes you will ever eat. In my youth, I was not a fan of meatloaf. Recipes like this changed my mind. If you are not a fan, I'll bet it will change your mind, too. If you can't get venison, substitute ground veal or turkey. Never cook meatloaf in a loaf pan. Meatloaf should always be cooked on a baking sheet with raised sides so that the fat drains away from the finished product. Cook meatloaf to just medium-well, no more, no less. All of the pink should be gone, but if you overcook it, it will be dry and tasteless. The glaze is key to the success of this recipe.

1 tablespoon bacon grease (or canola oil)
1 cup onion, minced
¾ cup celery, minced
¾ cup bell pepper, minced
1 teaspoon garlic, minced
⅛ teaspoon dried thyme
¼ teaspoon dried oregano
2 teaspoons steak seasoning
1 tablespoon salt
1 cup milk
3 eggs
1 tablespoon Worcestershire sauce
½ cup ketchup
1 pound ground beef
½ pound ground venison
½ pound ground pork
1½ cup unseasoned coarse bread crumbs

Preheat oven to 325°.

Heat the bacon grease in a large skillet over medium heat. Sauté the vegetables with herbs, seasoning, and salt until tender. Allow to cool.

Combine milk, eggs, Worcestershire sauce, and ketchup and mix well. Place ground beef, venison, pork, cooled vegetables, and egg mixture into a large mixing bowl. Using your hands, squish the meatloaf until you have mixed everything together and all is well incorporated. Fold in the bread crumbs. Do not overmix.

Shape the meat mixture into the form of a loaf on a baking sheet and place in the oven. After 40 minutes of cooking, use a pastry brush to spread the glaze (recipe follows) over the entire meatloaf. Return to the oven and bake for 20 more minutes. Again, remove the meatloaf and brush another layer of the glaze over it. Return it once again to the oven and bake for 20 more minutes. Brush one final layer of the glaze on the meatloaf and cook for 10 more minutes. Remove the meatloaf and allow it to rest 15 minutes before serving.

Yield: 8–10 servings

TOMATO GLAZE

1 teaspoon bacon fat
1 tablespoon onion, minced
1 tablespoon garlic, minced
1 teaspoon salt
½ teaspoon dried basil
¼ teaspoon black pepper, freshly ground
3 tablespoons brown sugar
2 tablespoons tomato paste
½ cup chicken broth
2 tablespoons yellow mustard
1 tablespoon Worcestershire sauce
1 cup ketchup

Heat the bacon fat in a small skillet over a low heat. Cook the onions, garlic, and salt for 2–3 minutes. Add the basil, black pepper, and brown sugar. Cook for 3–4 minutes, stirring constantly to prevent the sugar from burning. Stir in remaining ingredients and simmer for 5–6 minutes, stirring occasionally.

Naked Ladies
One forgets their existence until suddenly there is pink everywhere. They aren't like other flowers. Spider lillies are in the amaryllis family and give Fall its own exoticism.

WATERS

Buttermilk-Cream Cheese Mashed Potatoes

I like my potatoes lumpy. For extra lumpy potatoes, use an old-fashioned potato masher and stop mashing while you think they're too lumpy.

5 large Idaho potatoes, peeled and cut into even-sized large chunks
water to cover potatoes
2 tablespoons + 1 teaspoon salt
¼ pound cold unsalted butter, cut into 1-inch cubes
½ cup cream cheese, cut into cubes
1 cup buttermilk, heated
¾ teaspoon white pepper, freshly ground
¼ cup fresh parsley, chopped

Place the first 2 tablespoons of salt in a pot with the water and potatoes. Cook potatoes over medium heat until fork tender. Do not overcook; they will break up and absorb the water, resulting in a watery and less tasteful final product. Drain off all excess water and allow potatoes to sit uncovered in the dry, warm pot for 2 minutes. This will eliminate any excess moisture.

If you aren't going to use an old-fashioned handheld potato masher, place potatoes in a mixing bowl. Using a whip attachment, whip the potatoes on medium speed, breaking up the large pieces. Add butter cubes and cream cheese cubes a few at a time and mix until well blended. Turn your mixer down to a low speed and add buttermilk, the teaspoon of salt, and white pepper. Fold in the parsley just before serving.

Yield: 6–8 servings

Creamed Spinach

I could eat spinach with every meal. Romano or Gruyére cheese can be substituted. The Parmesan Cream Sauce (recipe follows) has multiple uses, especially with cream-based pasta dishes. Only use freshly grated Parmesan cheese.

2 tablespoons olive oil
2 tablespoons garlic, minced
1½ cup whipping cream
1½ cups Parmesan Cream Sauce (recipe follows)
¾ cup Parmesan cheese
2 tablespoons hot sauce
1 tablespoon lemon juice
1 tablespoon Creole Seasoning (recipe page 21)
2 teaspoons salt
½ teaspoon black pepper, freshly ground
2 pounds spinach, frozen, thawed, and squeezed dry
10 ounces fresh spinach leaves, stems removed

In a large skillet, heat olive oil over medium heat and sauté garlic for 1–2 minutes, being careful not to brown. Add whipping cream and bring to a simmer. Let this cook down for 3–4 minutes. Whisk in Parmesan Cream Sauce. Continue to cook, reducing mixture until it becomes thick. Add the Parmesan cheese, hot sauce, lemon juice, Creole seasoning, salt, and pepper.

Place fresh spinach leaves and frozen spinach in a large bowl and pour hot mixture over spinach. Using a large rubber spatula or spoon, stir well, incorporating the cream and spinach. Return it to the skillet and cook for 5–6 more minutes, or until spinach is thoroughly heated. Serve immediately.

Yield: 6–8 servings

PARMESAN CREAM SAUCE

1 quart heavy cream
½ pound Parmesan cheese, grated
⅓ pound Romano cheese, grated
2 teaspoons white pepper
⅛ teaspoon nutmeg
3 tablespoons butter
¼ cup flour

Bring heavy cream to a boil. Add cheeses and stir well. Add pepper and nutmeg. Next, in a small sauté pan, make a roux by melting the butter over medium heat. Blend in the flour and cook for 4–5 minutes, stirring constantly to prevent the roux from browning. Using a wire whisk, add roux to the milk/cheese mixture and continue cooking until thickened, 3–4 minutes. Remove from the heat.

This sauce may be made and held in refrigeration for up to 1 week.

Yield: 1 quart

All the Leaves Aren't Brown
I love to look through the leaves when they are changing; there is an intermingling of colors that exists between green, red, and orange that is indescribable.

Corn on the Cob with a Twist

The corn steams inside the parchment in a mixture of butter and seasoning. Good for the grill, too.

8 ears fresh corn, husks and silk removed
⅓ cup unsalted butter, softened
1½ teaspoons kosher salt
1 teaspoon black pepper, freshly ground
¾ teaspoon Poultry Seasoning (recipe page 111)

Preheat oven to 325°.

Rub the softened butter completely over the surface of each ear of corn. Combine the salt, pepper, and poultry seasoning, and spread evenly over the buttered surface of each ear. Wrap each ear in a piece of wax paper, followed by a piece of aluminum foil. Twist the ends of aluminum foil to seal.

Place the wrapped corn on a baking sheet, large enough so that the ears of corn are not touching. Bake 20 minutes. Remove from oven, turn each ear over, and bake 15 minutes more. Remove from oven and keep wrapped until ready to serve.

Yield: 8 servings

The Ultimate Chocolate Cake
with Caramel Ribbon Ice Cream

The process of folding the caramel into the ice cream is a bit tricky, but to achieve ribbons, take your time.

CAKE

1¾ cups cake flour
¾ cup cocoa (preferably Dutch processed)
2 teaspoons baking soda
1 teaspoon baking powder
½ teaspoon kosher salt
2 eggs
2 cups sugar
¾ cup melted butter
1 cup buttermilk
1 cup brewed coffee, at room temperature
1 teaspoon vanilla extract

Preheat oven to 350°. Lightly butter 2 8-inch cake pans and line with parchment. Butter the parchment and flour the pans, shaking out the excess.

Sift together flour, cocoa, baking soda, baking powder, and salt. Reserve.

Using a mixer with a whip attachment, beat eggs and sugar until thick and lemon-colored. Beat in the melted butter. Alternately add dry ingredients with buttermilk, scraping the bowl once or twice. Add the coffee and vanilla to form a thin batter. Divide batter between prepared cake pans.

Bake until a toothpick inserted in the center of the cake comes out clean, 40–45 minutes. Cool in pan for 15 minutes. Invert onto cooling racks, peel off paper, and cool completely.

When cool, split each cake in half with a serrated slicing knife to form four thin layers. Freeze the layers for 1 hour before assembling the finished cake. Make the filling and icing (recipes follow) while the layers are freezing.

Place the first layer on a cake serving dish and spread a thin layer of the filling evenly over the cake. Repeat this process until you have the layers assembled. Spread the frosting over the top layer and around the sides.

Serve with Caramel Ribbon Ice Cream (recipe follows).
Yield: not enough!

FILLING

1½ cups semisweet chocolate pieces
8 ounces cream cheese, softened
¾ cup powdered sugar

Place chocolate in a double boiler and heat until completely melted. While the chocolate melts, use an electric mixer with a wire whip attachment to beat together the cream cheese and powdered sugar. Beat until mixture is light and fluffy. Allow the melted chocolate to cool slightly, then drizzle it into the cream cheese mixture and continue beating until the filling is cool. This spreads best if used immediately.

ICING

6 ounces unsweetened chocolate
½ cup unsalted butter, softened
4 cups powdered sugar
1 cup sour cream
1 tablespoon vanilla extract

Melt the chocolate over a double boiler. Use an electric mixer with a wire whip attachment to cream together the butter and powdered sugar. Add the melted chocolate, sour cream, and vanilla extract and beat until light and fluffy. As with the filling, this spreads best if used immediately.

Caramel Ribbon Ice Cream

CARAMEL

1 cup sugar
¼ cup water
1½ cups heavy whipping cream, heated

In a small, heavy-duty saucepan, combine the sugar and water. Bring the mixture to a slow boil, stirring very often. Continue to cook until the mixture reaches a deep caramel color, about 10 minutes. As soon as this deep color is achieved, use a wire whisk and quickly stir in the warm cream. Return the caramel to a medium heat, and cook for 2–3 more minutes. Remove and cool the caramel completely. Set aside. The caramel should be thick but not completely stiff when cooled.

ICE CREAM

1 vanilla bean
2 cups heavy cream
2 cup milk
1½ cups sugar, divided
5 egg yolks

Split the vanilla bean lengthwise and combine it with heavy cream, milk, and half of the sugar in a small saucepan. Heat just until it begins to boil.

In a bowl whisk egg yolks with the remaining sugar. Beat until the egg yolks are light yellow in color. While whisking stream in about <⅓> of the boiled cream mixture. Add the yolk mixture to the remaining warm cream and cook for 5 more minutes over low heat, stirring constantly. Remove from heat and strain through a fine mesh strainer into a bowl set over ice. Cool mixture completely. Following the manufacturer's directions, freeze the mixture in an electric ice cream maker.

Place the finished ice cream in a chilled stainless steel bowl. Using a rubber spatula, fold the caramel into the ice cream. Try not to blend the caramel into the ice cream, but rather, create ribbons throughout.

Place in a freezer-safe sealable container and freeze until ready to use.

Yield: Approximately 2 quarts

Progressive Halloween Supper

Chili

Mexican Cornbread

Fish Tacos with Three Sauces

Seafood Nachos

Cajun Enchiladas

Crab Claws Geautreaux

Apple Cobbler

Cinnamon Ice Cream

Tricks are for Kids
Think back to a more innocent time when children and goblins filled the night air with promises of candy, apples, and ghost stories. Halloween has nearly been replaced by Harvest festivals. It's fun to make-believe.

Chili

My friend Beth Campbell hosts a group of families every Halloween. We have often offered to make it a progressive dinner, but Beth does such a great job entertaining, the kids and grown-ups return every year. One house—good friends and great food. Linda Nance makes my favorite chili. This is it.

1 tablespoon olive oil
1 tablespoon bacon fat
2 pounds beef sirloin, cut into ½-inch cubes
2½ teaspoons kosher salt
1½ teaspoons black pepper, freshly ground
3 cups yellow onion, medium dice
1 cup carrot, finely shredded
¼ cup fresh garlic, minced
1 tablespoon ground cumin
2 teaspoons ground coriander
1 teaspoon oregano
1½ tablespoons chili powder
1 6-ounce can tomato paste
2 28-ounce cans diced tomatoes
1 quart V-8 juice
1 quart hot chicken broth
2 bay leaves
2 14-ounce cans kidney beans, drained and rinsed
2 tablespoons corn flour
½ cup water
1 tablespoon fresh lime juice
¼ cup fresh cilantro, chopped

Heat the oil and bacon fat in an 8-quart, heavy-duty saucepan over high heat. Sprinkle the meat with salt and black pepper. Place half of the meat in the very hot oil. To achieve a nice golden brown sear, *do not move the meat for 3–4 minutes.* Turn the meat over and brown the other side the best that you can. Remove meat with a slotted spoon and place on a paper towel to drain. Repeat this process with the remaining meat.

Turn the heat to medium and add onion, carrot, and garlic. Cook 3–4 minutes. Using a wooden spoon, stir in the spices and tomato paste. Cook 10 minutes, stirring constantly to prevent burning. This step is very important. Caramelizing the sugars in the tomato paste and vegetables is what makes the difference in the outcome of the chili.

Return the meat to the pot. Add the canned tomatoes, V-8 juice, chicken broth, and bay leaves. Simmer slowly for 2–3 hours. Stir often to prevent sticking. Add the beans and simmer for 15 minutes more.

Combine the corn flour with the water to make a paste. Turn up the heat so that the chili reaches a slow boil and stir in the corn flour mixture. Allow the chili to cook for 5 minutes more. Remove from heat and stir in the lime juice and cilantro.

Yield: 1 gallon

Boo Radleys

In *To Kill a Mockingbird* a mysterious character would put toys and trinkets in the knot of a tree for Scout to find. He was the quintessential eccentric southerner, the hero in wolf's clothing.

Mexican Cornbread

Add more or less jalapeño depending on your heat tolerance. Leftover Mexican cornbread makes a great stuffing or Southwestern-flavored dressing to be served with roasted chicken. You can also cut the leftover cornbread into cubes and heat for a few hours in a low-heat oven for croutons in a Tex-Mex salad.

1 cup cornmeal
½ cup flour
¼ cup corn flour
2 teaspoons baking powder
½ teaspoon baking soda
½ teaspoon ground cumin
1 teaspoon chili powder
1½ teaspoons salt
1 egg
1 tablespoon bacon grease, melted (or canola oil)
¾ cup buttermilk
1 cup milk
1 cup freshly scraped corn kernels (or frozen corn kernels, thawed)
¼ cup green onions, thinly sliced
2 tablespoons jalapeño, minced

Preheat oven to 350°.

In a mixing bowl, combine cornmeal, flour, corn flour, baking powder, baking soda, cumin, chili powder, and salt and mix well. In a separate bowl, combine the egg, bacon grease, buttermilk, and milk and stir well. Fold the wet ingredients into the dry ingredients. Add the corn, green onions, and jalepeño and mix well. Do not over-mix. Pour batter into a greased cast-iron skillet or a buttered 2-quart baking dish and bake for 20–25 minutes.

Yield: 8 servings

Isle of Cypress
The color of Autumn is expressed well in the foliage of this cypress tree. They grow well in water and this one is also a home for Wood Ducks.

Fish Tacos with Three Sauces

The quality of the tortillas is key. If you have the time to make your own, go for it.

2 teaspoons cumin
1 teaspoon coriander
1 teaspoon chili powder
1 teaspoon granulated garlic
2 teaspoons kosher salt
⅛ teaspoon cayenne pepper
2 pounds mahi mahi filets (6–8 ounces each)
¼ cup canola oil

Combine seasonings. Sprinkle fish with seasoning, cover, and refrigerate for 1 hour.

In a medium-sized skillet, heat oil over medium heat. Add the fish to the skillet and cook 4–5 minutes on each side. Allow the fish to cool slightly then cut into thin strips.

To serve:
Set out the cooked fish and prepared salsas along with:

1½ cups green cabbage, shredded
1½ cups red cabbage, shredded
24 corn tortillas

Have guests spread the Chipotle Crème Fraiche (recipe follows) in the middle of a tortilla. Place 2 fish filet strips in each tortilla, add a small amount of the shredded cabbage, and top with one of the salsas.

Yield: tacos for 6–8 people

CHIPOTLE CRÈME FRAICHE

1 cup heavy whipping cream
2 teaspoons lemon juice
¼ cup sour cream
1 tablespoon chipotle peppers in adobe sauce, minced
½ teaspoon salt

Combine the heavy whipping cream and lemon juice in an airtight container and put it in a warm place for 6–8 hours. (It should be about 85°–95°.) Remove the cover and stir well. Refrigerate overnight.

After the crème fraiche has set up, stir in the sour cream, peppers, and salt. Store refrigerated until ready to serve.

FRESH FRUIT PICO DI GALLO

1 cup fresh tomatoes, small dice
¼ cup red onions, small dice
5 tablespoons cilantro, chopped
2 teaspoons fresh jalapeños, seeds removed and minced
½ cup pineapple, small dice
1 kiwi, peeled and small dice
½ cup orange segments
½ cup lime segments
½ teaspoon salt

Combine all ingredients together and refrigerate until ready to serve.

SWEET CORN AND BLACK BEAN SALSA

1 tablespoon olive oil
¼ cup yellow onion, minced
2 teaspoons garlic, minced
½ teaspoon salt
½ teaspoon cumin
¼ teaspoon coriander
⅛ teaspoon dry oregano
1 10-ounce can Rotel tomatoes
1 cup canned black beans, drained and rinsed
1 cup fresh sweet corn cut from the cob
¼ cup green onions, thinly sliced
2 teaspoons fresh lime juice
3 tablespoons cilantro, chopped

Place the olive oil in a small stainless steel saucepan over medium heat. Add the onion, garlic, salt, cumin, coriander, and oregano to the warm oil and cook 5 minutes, stirring often. Add Rotel tomatoes and allow mixture to simmer 2–3 minutes. Add black beans and corn and cook for 5 minutes more. Stir in the thinly sliced green onions, lime juice, and cilantro and remove from the heat.

Seafood Nachos

The cheese sauce should be made a day in advance and can be used as a stand-alone dip. The fried food should be cooked at the very last minute. This is a popular feature when we serve it in the Crescent City Grill.

CHEESE SAUCE

2 tablespoons olive oil
1 pound small shrimp, roughly chopped
¼ cup yellow onion, small dice
2 tablespoons green bell pepper, small dice
2 teaspoons fresh garlic, minced
2 teaspoons Creole Seasoning (recipe page 21)
½ teaspoon salt
2 teaspoons hot sauce
¾ cup half-and-half
½ pound Velveeta
1 pound cream cheese, softened
½ pound cheddar cheese, grated
½ pound lump crabmeat
2 teaspoons lemon juice

Heat oil in a medium saucepan over medium heat. Cook shrimp, onion, pepper, garlic, Creole Seasoning, and salt 7–8 minutes. Add hot sauce and half-and-half and bring to a simmer. Lower heat and add Velveeta and cream cheese. Stir until cheese has melted and remove from the heat. Add the grated cheddar and stir until melted. Gently fold in the crab and lemon juice.

FRIED TOPPINGS

Oil for frying
2 cups buttermilk
1 egg
2 cups corn flour
1 tablespoon salt
2 tablespoons Creole Seasoning (recipe page 21)
½ pound small shrimp
½ pound crawfish tails
1 cup sliced jalapeños

Preheat oven to 225°.

Heat oil to 340° in a large cast-iron skillet. Beat together the buttermilk and egg. Combine corn flour, salt, and Creole Seasoning. Individually dip shrimp, crawfish, and jalapeños into buttermilk mixture and then dredge in the corn flour mix. Shake off excess corn flour.

Fry ⅓–½ of the mixture for 5–6 minutes, until golden. Remove using a slotted spoon and drain on a paper towel–lined baking sheet. Place the cooked items in oven. Repeat the process until everything is fried.

To assemble:
1 large bag (1 pound bag) of your favorite tortilla chips, a large chip is best

Place about ⅓ of the chips on a large serving platter. Ladle ⅓ of the cheese sauce over the chips. Repeat this process until sauce is completely used. Top the nachos with the fried mixture and serve immediately.

Yield: 6–8 servings

Cajun Enchiladas

Try using a flavored tortilla for an added dimension. Great for a one-dish on a winter night.

½ cup butter, divided
½ cup yellow onion, small dice
½ cup canned jalapeños, drained and chopped fine
⅓ cup green bell pepper, small dice
1 tablespoon Creole Seasoning, divided (recipe page 21)
1½ cup whipping cream
½ cup sour cream
4 cups Monterey jack cheese, shredded and divided
½ pound fresh shrimp, 61–70 count
½ pound peeled crawfish tails
½ pound lump crabmeat
⅓ cup green onions, sliced thinly
8 8-inch flour tortillas

Preheat oven to 325°.

In a medium saucepan, melt half of the butter over medium-high heat. Cook the onions, jalapeños, bell pepper, and half of the Creole Seasoning 3–4 minutes, stirring often to prevent vegetables from browning. Add the whipping cream and bring mixture to a boil. Lower heat and simmer for 10 minutes, stirring constantly. Add the sour cream and half of the shredded cheese and stir with a wire whisk until the mixture is smooth. Remove from heat and pour mixture into a large mixing bowl. Set aside.

Melt the remaining butter in a large sauté pan over medium-high heat. Sprinkle the uncooked shrimp with the remaining Creole Seasoning and sauté 3–5 minutes. Add the crawfish tails, crab, and green onions and cook for 2 minutes more.

Fold the cooked seafood into the sour cream mixture.

Using a large spoon, place approximately ⅓ cup of the mixture into the center of each tortilla. Roll the tortillas and place them side by side in an 8 x 10-inch baking dish. Spoon the remaining mixture over the top of the filled tortillas. Cover the baking dish with a piece of parchment paper, followed by aluminum foil. With a small knife make 4–5 small slits in the foil.

Bake for 30 minutes. Remove the foil and parchment paper and sprinkle the top with the remaining shredded cheese and bake 10–12 minutes more. Allow the enchiladas to rest for 15 minutes before serving.

Yield: 6–8 servings

Ashes to Ashes
Local codes don't allow the burning of leaves anymore. Jumping across the fiery embers, scaring our parents, and going inside smelling of smoke was fun.

Crab Claws Geautreaux

Never use frozen crab claws. Fresh claws must be added at the last minute as they have already been cooked.

2 tablespoons olive oil
1½ tablespoons garlic, minced
1 teaspoon kosher salt
¼ cup white wine
½ cup chicken broth
1 cup Wishbone Italian Dressing
2 pounds fresh blue-crab fingers
1 teaspoon Creole Seasoning (recipe page 21)
½ teaspoon black pepper, freshly ground
¼ cup unsalted butter, cut into small cubes
2 tablespoons fresh parsley, chopped

Place the olive oil in a very large, heavy-duty sauté pan over low-medium heat. Place garlic and salt in the heated oil and cook 2–3 minutes, stirring constantly to prevent burning. Add the white wine, chicken broth, and Italian dressing and bring it to a simmer. Add the crab claws, Creole Seasoning, and black pepper and cook 4–5 minutes more, just until the crab is hot. Add the butter and parsley and gently stir until the butter is completely incorporated. Serve immediately.

Yield: 8–10 servings

Apple Cobbler

This recipe works with pears, too. Serve with a caramel ribbon ice cream for an added delight.

APPLE FILLING:

8 cups Granny Smith apples, peeled and sliced
½ cup sugar
¾ cup brown sugar
1½ teaspoons cinnamon
¼ teaspoon nutmeg
¼ cup flour
¼ teaspoon salt
1 teaspoon vanilla extract
½ cup water
2 tablespoons unsalted butter, softened, divided

In a large mixing bowl, combine apples, sugar, cinnamon, nutmeg, flour, salt, vanilla extract, and water. Using 1 tablespoon of butter, butter a 9 x 14-inch baking dish. Spread the apple mixture evenly into the prepared baking dish. Dot the tops of the apples with the remaining tablespoon of softened butter.

TOPPING:

1½ cup flour, sifted
1½ cup brown sugar
1½ teaspoons baking powder
¼ teaspoon salt
½ cup unsalted butter, softened
2 eggs, slightly beaten

Preheat oven to 375°.

Combine the sifted flour, brown sugar, baking powder, and salt and blend well. Blend in the butter and beaten egg. Drop the batter into 12 portions, over the apples, spacing the batter out evenly. Bake 30–40 minutes, until the apples are tender and the crust is golden brown. Remove from the oven and allow the cobbler to rest 15 minutes before serving.

Serve with Cinnamon Ice Cream (recipe follows).

Yield: 10–12 servings

Cinnamon Ice Cream

5 cups heavy cream
2½ cups whole milk
pinch salt
1½ cups sugar, divided
1 cinnamon stick
1 vanilla bean
12 large egg yolks

Combine the cream, milk, salt, ¾ cup of the sugar, and cinnamon stick in a large pot. Split the vanilla bean down the middle lengthwise and scrape out the seeds with a paring knife; add seeds to the pot and toss in the pods for extra flavor. Place the cream mixture over medium heat and bring to a simmer, stirring with a wooden spoon to dissolve the sugar. Cook 15 minutes, being careful that the mixture does not boil, simmer, or scald. Turn off the heat, cover the pot, and allow the cream mixture to steep for 15 minutes to further infuse the cinnamon and vanilla flavor.

In the meantime, with a wire whisk lightly blend the yolks in a large mixing bowl. Gradually add the remaining ¾ cup of sugar and continue to whisk until the sugar is dissolved completely and the eggs are thick and pale yellow, approximately 6 minutes.

Using a large ladle or measuring cup, temper the eggs by gradually whisking in 2 cups of the hot cream mixture. Return this back to the rest of the cream in the saucepan and turn heat to medium-low. Stir constantly until the custard thickens and leaves a path on the back of a spoon when you run your finger across it, approximately 10–12 minutes (do not allow to boil.)

Strain through a fine mesh strainer into a stainless steel mixing bowl and place bowl over an ice bath to chill completely. Stir the mixture while it is cooling. For best results, store the ice cream base overnight, covered, in the refrigerator.

Following the manufacturer's instructions of your ice cream freezer, prepare the ice cream. Transfer to airtight containers and freeze until needed.

Yield: ½ gallon

Thanksgiving

Roasted Turkey and Giblet Gravy

Deep South Cornbread Dressing

Cranberry Relish

Sweet Potatoes and Not a Marshmallow in Sight

Asparagus Casserole

Pumpkin Cheesecake

Roasted Turkey and Giblet Gravy

This recipe should be made a minimum of four times a year. Why wait until Thanksgiving to eat something that tastes so good?

brine (⅓ cup salt per gallon of water)
1 turkey, giblets reserved
1 onion
1 carrot
1 stalk of celery
1 tablespoon kosher salt
1 tablespoon black pepper, freshly ground
1 tablespoon Poultry Seasoning (recipe page 111)
2–3 cups chicken broth
¼ cup flour
1 tablespoon Kitchen Bouquet Brown and Seasoning Sauce

Dissolve salt in a small amount of hot water; add ice and cold water to equal one gallon. In an ice chest, place the thawed turkey and enough brine to completely submerge. For best results let turkey sit in cold brine (41° or below) for 24 hours.

Preheat oven to 300°.

Rough chop onion, carrot, and stalk of celery and place vegetables in cavity of turkey. Truss turkey. Sprinkle skin of the turkey with kosher salt, pepper, and poultry seasoning. Place turkey in a roasting pan on a roasting rack. Place 2 cups of chicken broth in the bottom of the roasting pan and place all in the oven. Roast turkey for 12 minutes per pound. Do not baste or open the oven door during cooking process.

When done (turkey has reached 180° on a meat thermometer inserted into the thickest part of the thigh), remove the roasting rack and place turkey on a cookie sheet.

Remove the drippings from the pan. Using a fat separator, remove fat from the broth. Place the turkey fat into a medium-sized skillet (you should have ¼ cup fat; if you do not, add a bit of oil to make up the difference). Chop the giblets into small pieces. Add the giblets to the hot fat and cook 5–6 minutes. Heat broth in a microwave. Add ¼ cup flour to the fat and giblets and cook over a medium heat for 4–5 minutes, stirring constantly. Incorporate the hot broth into the roux mixture and simmer until thickened. Add heated canned chicken broth if gravy is too thick. Add 1 tablespoon Kitchen Bouquet.

Let turkey rest for 2 minutes per pound before carving.

Yield: Feeds 1 hungry family and a few unwanted relatives

Indian Summer
The cornucopia has long represented abundance. The pilgrim, the turkey, and the horn of plenty vie for the number one spot as Thanksgiving mascot.

Deep South Cornbread Dressing

Make an extra batch and freeze it to be eaten in the winter months with roasted chicken. This is great as a stand-alone, center-of-the-plate dish topped with the gravy recipe from the turkey.

1 Cornish (game) hen
2 quarts chicken broth
½ onion
½ carrot
1 bay leaf
1 tablespoon bacon grease (or canola oil)
¼ cup bell pepper, diced
1 cup celery, diced
1 cup onion, diced
2 teaspoons celery salt
2 teaspoons Poultry Seasoning (recipe page 111)
2 cups Mushroom Béchamel Sauce (recipe follows)
2 cups heavy cream
1½ cups chicken broth, strained from cooking hen
4 eggs
1 recipe cornbread, crumbled
2 eggs, hard-boiled, chopped

Place the hen, broth, onion, carrot, and bay leaf in a medium stockpot. Simmer 1 hour and 20 minutes over medium heat. Remove hen and strain the broth. Allow hen to cool and pull meat from the bones. Chop meat.

Preheat oven to 325°.

In a medium skillet, melt bacon grease over low heat. Add bell pepper, celery, onion, celery salt, and poultry seasoning and cook slowly for 10 minutes.

Pour into a mixing bowl. Add Mushroom Béchamel Sauce, cream, broth, and eggs, mixing well. Add crumbled cornbread, boiled egg, and hen meat. Mix until all is well incorporated. Pour into a 3-quart baking dish. Bake 1 hour 15 minutes. Do not overcook dressing. It should be moist but not runny.

Yield: 8–12 servings

MUSHROOM BÉCHAMEL SAUCE

2 teaspoons light olive oil
2 tablespoons onion, minced
1 tablespoon shallot, minced

1 tablespoon celery, minced

½ teaspoon salt

3 ounces mushrooms, cleaned and sliced (1 cup)

1 cup chicken broth, heated

¼ teaspoon granulated garlic

⅛ teaspoon dried thyme

3 tablespoons cup butter

¼ cup flour

⅓ cup whipping cream, warm

Heat oil in a 3-quart saucepan over low heat. Add onion, shallot, celery, and salt. Cook vegetables until tender. Add mushrooms and increase heat to medium. Cook 10 minutes, stirring often. Add chicken broth, garlic, and thyme. Bring back to a simmer and cook 10 more minutes.

In a separate skillet, make a light-blond roux by melting butter and stirring in flour. Add to simmering broth mixture. Cook 3–4 minutes and add cream. Freezes well.

Yield: 3 cups

Reinventing the Wheel

The introduction of the mechanical tractor permanently replaced the mule and plough. Though the basic design has remained unchanged for years, newer models can come with enclosed cabs, air conditioning, CD players, and GPS systems.

Cranberry Relish

This is great served hot or cold, and makes a great condiment for leftover turkey sandwiches.

12-ounce bag fresh cranberries
¼ cup shallot, minced
1 cup Madeira wine
½ cup white sugar
½ cup brown sugar
¼ cup orange juice
¼ cup cranberry juice
2 teaspoons cornstarch
2 tablespoons cold water

Combine cranberries, shallot, Madeira, sugars, orange juice, and cranberry juice in a 1-quart saucepan and simmer over low-medium heat 20–30 minutes or until the cranberries become soft.

Separately, mix the cornstarch with the cold water then add to the cranberry mixture. Turn up heat to a heavy simmer and continue to cook, stirring well, for another 5–10 minutes.

Yield: 8–10 servings

Sweet Potatoes and
Not a Marshmallow in Sight

Your relatives that are die-hard marshmallow eaters will forget all about the dark side of sweet-potato casseroles and love this nut-topped version.

4 cups sweet potatoes, cooked, peeled, and mashed
1 cup sugar
½ cup honey
2 cup brown sugar, divided
4 eggs, beaten
1 cup heavy cream
3 sticks butter, divided
1 teaspoon cinnamon
1 teaspoon nutmeg
1 cup cornflakes
1 cup pecans, chopped
1 cup slivered almonds

Preheat oven to 350°.

Lightly butter a 13 x 9-inch casserole dish. Combine prepared sweet potatoes, sugar, honey, 1 cup of the brown sugar, eggs, cream, half of the butter, cinnamon, and nutmeg in a bowl; mix thoroughly. Place sweet potato mixture in the casserole dish.

Combine cornflakes, pecans, almonds, and remaining butter and brown sugar in a bowl. Mix until crumbly. Sprinkle over sweet potato mixture.

Bake 40–45 minutes or until center is hot.

Yield: 10–12 servings

Asparagus Casserole

Substitute broccoli and ham or bacon for the asparagus. Green beans, zucchini, or English peas would work well, too.

1 tablespoon olive oil, light
2 tablespoons onion, minced
1 tablespoon shallot, minced
2 tablespoons celery, minced
½ teaspoon salt
2 cups mushrooms, cleaned and sliced
1½ cups chicken broth
½ teaspoon granulated garlic
⅛ teaspoon dried thyme
¼ cup butter
⅓ cup flour
½ cup whipping cream
1 teaspoon Worcestershire sauce
1 teaspoon hot sauce
2 bunches fresh asparagus, cut on a bias into 2½-inch-long pieces
½ cup Parmesan cheese
½ cup white cheddar cheese, shredded
2 tablespoons fresh parsley
3 tablespoons unsalted butter, melted
1½ cups Ritz crackers crushed into crumbs (about 35 crackers)

Preheat oven to 350°.

Heat oil in a 2-quart saucepan over low heat. Add onion, shallot, celery, and salt. Cook vegetables until tender. Add mushrooms and increase heat to medium. Cook 10 minutes, stirring often. Add chicken broth, garlic, and thyme. Bring back to a simmer and cook 10 minutes more.

In a separate skillet, make a light-blond roux by melting butter and stirring in flour. Add to simmering broth mixture. Cook 3–4 minutes and add cream. Add Worcestershire sauce and hot sauce.

While sauce is cooking, bring 2 quarts of water mixed with 1 tablespoon salt to a boil. Cook the asparagus 1 minute. Drain and run asparagus under cold water until cool. Using paper towels, dry the asparagus completely.

In a mixing bowl, combine asparagus with the sauce, cheddar and Parmesan cheeses, and parsley. Place the mixture in a 2½-quart baking dish and bake 20 minutes.

Combine the melted butter and cracker crumbs. Spread crumb mixture over the top of the casserole and bake 10 minutes more. Allow casserole to set 10 minutes before serving.

Yield: 8 servings

Pumpkin Cheesecake

This is a fall staple in the Crescent City Grill, but we receive requests for the recipe year round. A spring-form pan is a must.

1½ pounds cream cheese, room temperature
1 cup brown sugar
pinch salt
5 eggs
4 egg yolks
2 teaspoons vanilla extract
1½ cups pumpkin puree
1 teaspoon cinnamon
¼ teaspoon nutmeg
⅛ teaspoon allspice

Preheat the oven to 275°.

Place softened cream cheese in a large mixing bowl and beat using paddle attachment on medium speed until *very* smooth. Scrape sides and beat again to ensure there are no lumps. Add sugar and salt and mix well. Add eggs and yolks a few at a time, allowing them to incorporate well before adding more. Set the mixer to low and add vanilla, pumpkin puree, cinnamon, nutmeg, and allspice. Blend well another 2–3 minutes.

CRUST

2¼ cups graham cracker crumbs
1 teaspoon cinnamon
½ cup sugar
¾ cup melted butter

Combine crumbs, cinnamon, and sugar and mix by hand. Add butter in stages, mixing well before each addition.

Evenly distribute the crust in a 10-inch spring-form pan, pressing it firmly on the bottom of the pan and building crust up 2 inches on the sides.

Pour in the cheesecake batter and bake 1–1½ hours. The cheesecake should jiggle slightly when tapped. Remove and refrigerate overnight before serving.

To cut, run a thin knife under hot water before cutting each slice.

Yield: 10–14 servings

Christmas Eve Dinner

Pork Tenderloin with Muscadine Glaze

Beef Tenderloin
with Horseradish-Spiked Bordelaise Sauce

Oyster Dressing

Sweet Potato Stuffed Oranges

Spinach Soufflé

Grand Marnier Crème Brulée

Circle on the Square
Small town Christmas decorations are hung on streetlamps to herald the buying season. Thanksgiving is the official start, but it seems to arrive earlier each year.

PAGES 182–183:
On Top of Old Smoky
This section of the Blue Ridge is known for the color of its mountains in the distance. The park opened three hours before I did this painting, and the snow was still fresh on the ground.

Pork Tenderloin
with Muscadine Glaze

This might be my favorite recipe in the book. It is simple, it is original, and it is extremely tasty. It's also great for bringing to a friend's house.

4 pork tenderloins (approximately 10 ounces each)
2 teaspoons kosher salt
1 teaspoon black pepper, freshly ground
2 tablespoons olive oil
1 tablespoon unsalted butter
2 tablespoons shallot, minced
½ teaspoon garlic, minced
¼ teaspoon salt
¼ cup brown sugar
½ cup Riesling wine, or muscadine wine, if you can find it
¼ cup balsamic vinegar
1 cup chicken broth
1 bay leaf
¾ cup muscadine jelly
¼ teaspoon black pepper, freshly ground
¼ cup red bell pepper, minced
2 tablespoons fresh parsley, chopped

Season the pork with the salt and pepper.

In an ovenproof skillet, heat the olive oil over high heat. Once the oil is hot, add the butter and the pork tenderloins. Sear each tenderloin on all sides and place all (the skillet and tenderloins) in the oven. Cook 8–10 minutes.

Remove the skillet from the oven and place the tenderloins on a plate and hold in a warm place. Drain excess oil from the skillet, reserving 1 tablespoon.

Place the skillet over low heat. Cook shallot, garlic, and salt for 2–3 minutes. Add the brown sugar and cook until the sugar is melted. Turn the heat to medium and add the wine and balsamic vinegar. Cook until the mixture has reduced by half. Add the chicken broth and bay leaf and simmer until the mixture has reduced by 70 percent. Stir in the jelly, black pepper, and red pepper and simmer 5–6 minutes more, stirring often to prevent sticking and burning. Remove from heat and stir in the fresh parsley.

Cut each tenderloin—by slicing on a diagonal—into 6–8 pieces. Arrange the slices on a serving platter and pour the glaze over the pork. Serve immediately.

Yield: 6–8 servings

Beef Tenderloin with Horseradish-Spiked Bordelaise Sauce

I grew up eating turkey on Christmas Eve. This recipe, along with the pork tenderloin, has changed the course of our family holiday dinners forever. If you don't have veal stock, substitute a high-quality veal demi-glace, a veal or beef base combined with water, or low-sodium beef broth.

3 sprigs fresh thyme
¼ cup olive oil
5 pounds beef tenderloin, cleaned
2 teaspoons kosher salt
2 teaspoons black pepper, freshly ground

Preheat oven to 400°.

Remove the leaves from the thyme sprigs and chop the thyme. Add the thyme to the oil and rub the outside of the beef tenderloin with the mixture. Sprinkle the tenderloin with the salt and pepper. Place a large heavy-duty skillet over high heat. When the skillet is very hot, sear the tenderloin 3–4 minutes on each side. Place the tenderloin on a baking rack inside of a roasting pan, and place it in the preheated oven. Roast until the internal temperature is 125° (for medium rare), approximately 30–40 minutes. Remove from the oven and allow the meat to rest for 15 minutes before slicing and serving.

HORSERADISH-SPIKED BORDELAISE

2 tablespoons unsalted butter
½ cup yellow onion, small dice
⅓ cup carrot, peeled, small dice
¼ cup celery, small dice
2 teaspoons garlic, minced
½ teaspoon salt
2 tablespoons tomato paste
½ teaspoon black pepper, freshly ground
1 cup dry red wine
1 bay leaf
1 quart veal stock (or rich beef stock)
3 tablespoons prepared horseradish
1 teaspoon fresh thyme leaves, chopped

Heat the butter in a 2-quart saucepan over medium heat. Place the onion, carrot, celery, garlic, and salt in the heated pot and cook until vegetables soften, approximately 5–6 minutes. Add the tomato paste and black pepper, stirring constantly for 5–6 minutes. Using a wire whisk, add the red wine and bay leaf. Simmer until the wine has reduced by half. Add the veal stock and bring to a boil. Reduce the heat to low-medium and simmer very slowly until reduced by half (approximately 1–1½ hours).

Adjust the seasoning and hold warm until ready to serve. Stir in the horseradish and fresh thyme just before serving.

To serve the tenderloin, slice the beef into ¾-inch slices and arrange on a serving platter. Pour half of the sauce over the beef and place the remaining sauce in a gravy boat on the table.

Yield: 8–12 servings

The Buck Stops Here
The holidays offer two religious
Events: the birth of the Savior and
deer season. I was always relieved
when my uncle came back from
hunting without Rudolph.

Oyster Dressing

My brother-in-law once brought an oyster dressing to a holiday dinner at our home. It was green. Extremely green. This is not his recipe.

¼ cup unsalted butter
2 ounces andouille sausage, very small dice
¾ cups yellow onion, small dice
¾ cups celery, small dice
2 tablespoons red bell pepper, fine dice
1 teaspoon garlic, minced
¼ teaspoon salt
¼ teaspoon Poultry Seasoning (recipe page 111)
½ teaspoon black pepper, freshly ground
1 teaspoon dried sage
2 tablespoons fresh parsley, chopped
3 cups chicken broth
3 large eggs
2 cups oysters, shucked
3 slices white bread, dried in a warm oven and crumbled
1½ cups day-old cornbread, crumbled
6 saltine crackers, crumbled

Preheat oven to 350°.

Melt the butter in a large sauté pan over medium heat. Add the sausage and cook 5–6 minutes. Add onions and celery and cook 5–10 minutes, stirring often to prevent browning. Add red bell pepper, garlic, salt, poultry seasoning, black pepper, and sage. Continue cooking for 3 minutes more.

Remove mixture from the heat and place in a large mixing bowl. Add chopped parsley, chicken broth, and eggs, beating well with a wire whisk until well blended. Fold in the oysters, crumbled white bread, cornbread, and crackers. Pour into a 3-quart Pyrex baking dish and bake 45 minutes. Remove from the oven, allow to sit 10 minutes, and serve.

Yield: 8–10 servings

Sweet Potato Stuffed Oranges

This is a variation of a dish my mother made for every Christmas Eve of my childhood. They look great on the plate.

2 cups * sweet potatoes, cooked, peeled, and mashed (2–3 sweet potatoes)
½ cup brown sugar
2 eggs, beaten
¼ cup heavy cream
¼ butter, softened
½ teaspoon cinnamon
¼ teaspoon nutmeg
2 teaspoons orange zest
5 large oranges, cut in half and scooped out
1 tablespoon fresh chives, thinly sliced
½ cup toasted almond slices

Preheat oven to 350°.

Combine hot sweet potatoes, brown sugar, eggs, cream, butter, cinnamon, nutmeg, and orange zest in a bowl; mix thoroughly. Place the hollowed out orange halves on a lined baking sheet. Fill each half with the sweet potato mixture.

Bake 20–25 minutes. Just before serving, sprinkle each serving with the sliced chives and toasted almonds.

Yield: 8–10 servings

* To cook the sweet potatoes: Preheat oven to 375°. Place the whole potatoes on a baking sheet and roast for 20–30 minutes. Turn each potato over once midway through the cooking time. Allow the potatoes to cool slightly so that they are easier to handle when peeling. Simply place the peeled sweet potatoes into a stainless steel mixing bowl and mash them using a stiff wire whisk or potato masher.

Spinach Soufflé

If you chop the spinach you can use this recipe as a dip.

⅓ cup butter
¼ cup shallot, minced
2 teaspoons garlic, minced
⅓ cup flour
½ teaspoon Creole Seasoning (recipe page 21)
½ teaspoon salt
¼ teaspoon black pepper, freshly ground
⅛ teaspoon ground nutmeg
1⅓ cup milk, heated
2 teaspoons hot sauce
4 large eggs, separated
2 10-ounce packages frozen spinach (thaw and squeeze out as much water as possible)
½ teaspoon cream of tartar
2 tablespoons unsalted butter, softened

Preheat oven to 350°.

Heat butter in a 2-quart saucepan over medium heat. Cook shallot and garlic for 3 minutes. Blend in flour and cook 4–5 minutes, stirring often to prevent burning. Add Creole Seasoning, salt, pepper, and nutmeg and blend well. Gradually add the warm milk, stirring constantly with a wire whisk. Remove from heat and stir in the hot sauce.

In a small bowl, beat the egg yolks until light and frothy. Fold the yolks into the sauce mixture. Add the spinach to the sauce mixture.

Using the whip attachment on an electric mixer, beat the egg whites with cream of tartar until stiff peaks form. Stir ¼ of the stiff egg whites into the spinach mixture. Gently fold in the remaining egg whites.

Butter a 2-quart round Pyrex baking dish. Pour the spinach mixture into prepared baking dish. Place the Pyrex dish in a water bath with 2 inches of water. Bake for 1 hour and serve immediately.

Yield: 8–10 servings

Grand Marnier Crème Brulée

Must be made a day in advance. Be careful when caramelizing the sugar. If it burns, you'll have to start all over again.

2 cups heavy whipping cream
2 cups half-and-half
½ vanilla bean, split in half lengthwise
1 cup sugar, divided
10 egg yolks
¼ cup Grand Marnier
½ cup sugar to caramelize the tops of the crème brulée

Preheat oven to 300°.

In a heavy-bottomed, non-reactive saucepan, heat the cream, half-and-half, vanilla bean, and half of the sugar over medium heat. Allow mixture to cook 5 minutes, being careful not to boil over.

Using an electric mixer, beat the egg yolks on high speed until light and fluffy. Gradually add in the remaining half a cup of sugar. Add the Grand Marnier. Set the mixer to low speed and slowly add 1 cup of the hot cream mixture. Then, using a rubber spatula, slowly blend in the remaining hot cream mixture. Allow the mixture to settle for 5 minutes.

Using a small ladle or large serving spoon, skim the frothy bubbles from the top of the mixture. Divide the custard into 8 (8–ounce) ramekins or custard cups. Place the dishes into a large roasting pan. Pour enough hot water in the roasting pan so that the water level is halfway up the sides of the custard dishes.

Bake 35–40 minutes, or until the middle is set. The custard should jiggle slightly.

Remove custards from the roasting pan and cool completely.

Twenty minutes before serving, remove the custards from the refrigerator. Sprinkle the sugar in a thin layer over the top of each custard dish, covering it completely. To caramelize, light a propane torch and hold it so the flame just touches the surface. Start in the center and, moving the torch in a spiral pattern, cook the sugar until it becomes light brown in color. Serve immediately.

Yield: 8 servings

Christmas Morning Breakfast

Christmas Morning Casserole

Orange Country Ham

Garlic Cheese Grits

Andouille in Blankets

Mary Virginia's Orange Sweet Rolls

Cinnamon Rolls

Southern Gothic
Watermelons have a red and green
color scheme. So does Christmas. Why?
Simply put, Claus.

WATERS

Christmas Morning Casserole

Of the four breakfast casseroles I have created for cookbooks, this one is my wife's favorite. You're busy enough on Christmas Eve and Christmas morning, so make the casserole two days ahead of time and hold, covered, in the refrigerator.

1 pound bacon, good quality, medium dice
¾ cup onion, diced
1 cup fresh mushrooms, very thinly sliced
½ cup red bell pepper, medium dice
½ cup green onion, thinly sliced
1 teaspoon garlic
1 teaspoon Creole Seasoning (recipe page 21)
1 teaspoon cayenne pepper
10 eggs, beaten
1 cup half-and-half
1 teaspoon dry mustard
10 small biscuits, crumbled, (3–4 cups)
4 ounces brie cheese, rind removed and cut into small pieces
1 cup Romano cheese, shredded
1 teaspoon hot sauce

Preheat oven to 325°.

Brown bacon in a large skillet and drain most of the fat. Add onion, mushrooms, bell pepper, green onion, garlic, Creole Seasoning, and cayenne and cook 5 minutes. Set aside.

Combine the eggs, half-and-half, and dry mustard in a mixing bowl. Fold the crumbled biscuits, cheeses, and the bacon mixture into the eggs. Add the hot sauce. Mix well and place in a buttered 2-quart baking dish. Bake for 40–50 minutes. Allow to rest for 15 minutes before serving.

Yield: 8–10 servings

Orange Country Ham

Bold and salty, good stuff. Make sure to use unsalted butter because the ham is salty enough. Freshly squeezed orange juice is key.

2 tablespoons unsalted butter
1½ pounds country ham, sliced ⅛–¼-inch thick
¼ cup orange juice, freshly squeezed
2 tablespoons orange marmalade
¼ cup pure maple syrup
1½ teaspoons black pepper, freshly ground

Melt half of the butter in a large heavy-duty skillet over medium-high heat. Just as it begins to brown, place the ham slices in the skillet. Brown each side and place ham on a baking sheet. Repeat this process to brown the remaining ham.

Lower the heat and place the orange juice, marmalade, and maple syrup in the ham skillet. Cook 4–5 minutes, stirring often to prevent burning. Add the ham back into the skillet along with the black pepper. Use a pair of tongs to move the ham and coat each slice with the glaze. When the ham is coated and hot, remove from the heat and serve immediately.

Yield: 6–8 servings

Garlic Cheese Grits

Never use instant grits. If you want this dish spicier, use pepper-jack cheese. Made correctly, and stored, covered, the grits will hold warm for an hour or two.

1 tablespoon bacon grease or oil
1 tablespoon garlic, minced
1 teaspoon salt
2 cups milk
2 cups chicken broth
1 cup grits
1 teaspoon Creole Seasoning (recipe page 21)
1 teaspoon hot sauce
8 ounces sharp cheddar cheese, shredded
4 ounces cream cheese

Melt bacon grease over low heat in a 1½-quart saucepan. Add garlic and salt and cook for 1–2 minutes, being careful not to brown the garlic. Add milk and broth and increase heat. Bring to a simmer and slowly pour in grits. Lower heat and cook grits 15 minutes, stirring often. Add remaining ingredients and stir until cheeses are melted. Serve immediately.

Yield: 8 servings

Past Present

You never know what's inside a Christmas present. As a small kid the wrapping paper was its own gift. But mostly, it was a way to make us think that there was something special about socks.

Andouille in Blankets

Make sure you are using top quality cheese and sausage. If you don't like the spiciness of andouille, substitute your favorite smoked sausage or even kielbasa. You might want to make a few of these on Christmas Eve to leave by the fireplace for Santa. He's likely to be full of cookies and milk by the time he arrives at your house.

4 andouille sausages (approximately 1 pound)
1 tablespoon bacon grease
½ cup yellow onion, minced
2 tablespoons green bell pepper, very small dice
2 tablespoons red bell pepper, very small dice
2 tablespoons celery, very small dice
2 teaspoons garlic, minced
1 teaspoon Creole Seasoning (recipe page 21)
2 packages Pillsbury crescent rolls

Preheat oven to 350°.

Using a sharp knife, cut the sausages into quarters, lengthwise. You should have 16 4–5-inch-long, narrow pieces.

In a small sauté pan, melt the bacon fat over medium heat. Cook the onions, peppers, and celery 3–4 minutes. Add the garlic and Creole Seasoning and cook for 3–4 minutes more. Remove from the heat and cool.

Spoon 1 teaspoon of the vegetable mixture down the center of each crescent roll. Place a piece of sausage on each prepared crescent roll and wrap the dough around the sausage.

Bake until golden brown.

Yield: 16 pieces

Mary Virginia's Orange Sweet Rolls

Mary Virginia McKenzie was my across-the-street neighbor for 18 years. She's a great cook. She makes these sweet rolls every Saturday morning. That, alone, is reason to love the street I grew up on. I can safely say that I have eaten these sweet rolls every Christmas morning for my entire life. They're good year-round. They freeze well.

1 cup boiling water
1 cup shortening (or 2 sticks of butter)
1 cup sugar
1½ teaspoons salt
2 eggs (large)
2 tablespoons yeast (2 packages)
1 cup warm water
dash sugar
6 cups flour
1 stick butter, melted
1¼ cup granulated sugar
1½ tablespoons cinnamon
1 pound confectioner's sugar
grated rind of 2 navel oranges
enough orange juice to make a glaze

Pour boiling water over shortening, sugar, and salt. Blend and let cool. Add eggs and beat well.

Let yeast stand in warm water with a dash of sugar until bubbly. Add yeast mixture to shortening mixture when it is absolutely cool. Then beat in the flour. Cover and refrigerate 3–4 hours.

Preheat oven to 350°. Using melted butter, grease 6 aluminum-foil–lined 9-inch cake pans.

Roll out dough into a large rectangle (1 foot by 3 feet). Sprinkle with granulated sugar and cinnamon. Roll up dough, jellyroll style, from the long side. Cut ½-inch-thick and place rolls into prepared cake pans. Let rise until doubled in size (about 1 hour). Bake 15 minutes.

Make a glaze using confectioner's sugar, orange rind, and orange juice. Ice rolls while they are hot.

Yield: 6 tins (not enough)

Cinnamon Rolls

Humidity dictates the amount of milk needed in the icing. Down here we use less milk.

1 cup boiling water
1 cup shortening (or 2 sticks of butter)
1 cup sugar
1½ teaspoons salt
2 eggs (large)
2 tablespoons yeast (2 packages)
1 cup warm water
dash sugar
6 cups flour
½ cup melted butter
1 cup raisins
½ cup brown sugar
½ cup sugar
1½ tablespoons cinnamon
1 pound confectioner's sugar
1 teaspoon cinnamon
2–4 tablespoons milk

Preheat oven to 350°.

Pour boiling water over shortening, sugar, and salt. Blend and let cool. Add eggs and beat well.

Let yeast stand in warm water with a dash of sugar until bubbly. When the yeast-water mixture has cooled completely add to shortening mixture, then beat in the flour. Cover and refrigerate 3–4 hours.

Using melted butter, grease 6 aluminum-foil–lined 9-inch cake pans.

Roll out dough into a large rectangle (1 foot by 3 feet). Using a pastry brush, coat the entire surface of the dough with the melted butter. Distribute the raisins evenly over the buttered dough.

Combine the brown sugar, sugar, and cinnamon and sprinkle the surface of the dough with this mixture.

Roll up dough, jellyroll style, from the long side. Cut into ¾-inch-thick segments and place into prepared cake pans. Let rise until doubled in size (about 1 hour).

Bake for 15 minutes.

Combine the confectioner's sugar, cinnamon, and milk to make the icing. Ice rolls while they are hot.

Yield: a ton

Classical Gas

One of my earliest memories is playing on the floor looking into a space heater. Like Our Lady of the Perpetual Space Heater, it gave me pause to wonder.

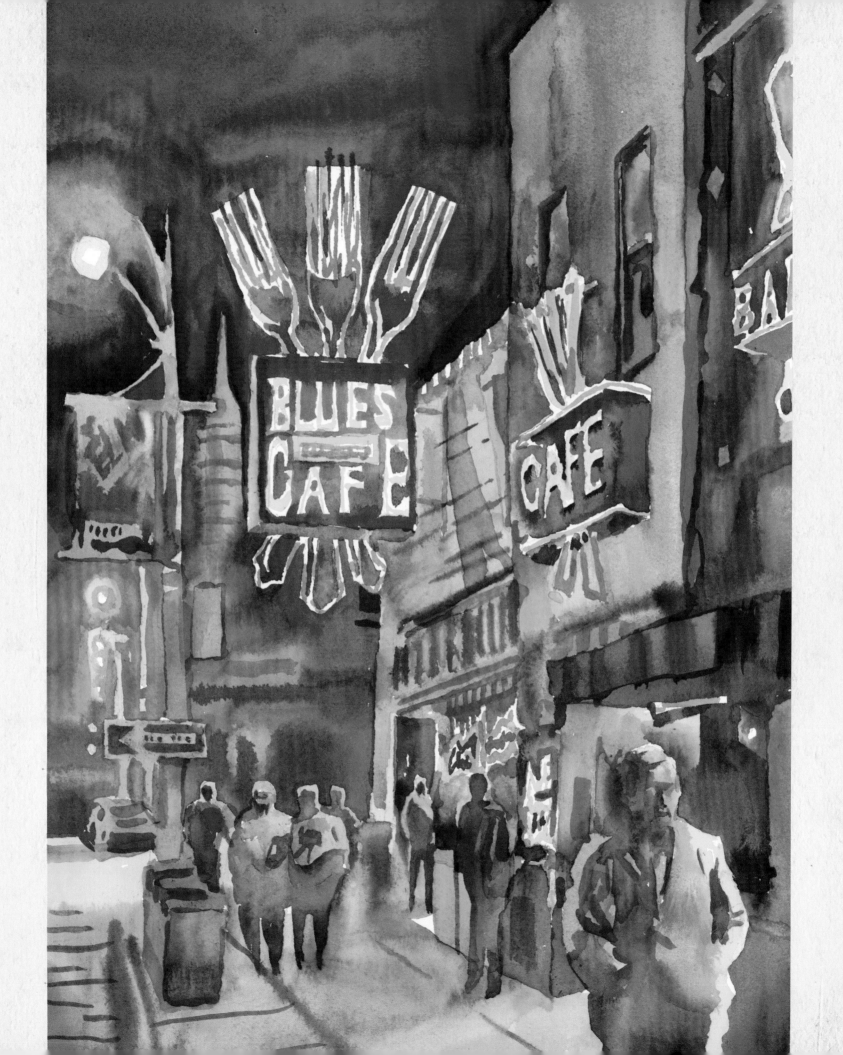

New Year's Eve Dinner

Foie Gras with Toasted Brioche, Fig Relish,
and Reduced Port Wine Glaze

Frisee and Warm Mushroom Salad

Lobster and Brie Bisque

Lamb Chops with Mint Compound Butter

Au Gratin Potatoes

Chocolate Croissant Bread Pudding

Bourbon Crème Anglaise

Walking in Memphis
The blues and other colors are
here. Neon lights, loud music, and the
smell of fried food give a psychedelic
effect on Beale Street in Memphis.

Foie Gras with Toasted Brioche, Fig Relish, and Reduced Port Wine Glaze

If you have a well-connected gourmet butcher, have him special order a small lobe of foie gras. Ask him how to clean and cut it as I don't have the space on this page. If you can't purchase foie gras through your local butcher, ask the chef at your favorite white-tablecloth restaurant. This recipe will be well worth the effort. The relish is best if made a day or two in advance.

1 pound foie gras cut into 2-ounce slices
1½ teaspoons kosher salt
¼ teaspoon black pepper, freshly ground
8 slices fresh Brioche, ⅓-inch thick, crusts removed and cut in half on a diagonal
1 recipe Fig Relish
1 recipe Port Wine Glaze

Preheat oven to 450°.

Season the foie gras with the salt and black pepper. Heat a large nonstick skillet over high heat and arrange the foie gras in the heated skillet so they are not touching. Cook 45 seconds. Turn each piece over and cook 1–2 minutes. Turn off the heat.

Arrange the Brioche (recipe follows) on a baking sheet. Place the brioche in the oven to toast.

To serve, place 1 piece of the brioche toast on each serving plate, top with 1 piece of the cooked foie gras. Top each piece of foie gras with 2 teaspoons of the Fig Relish (recipe follows). Rest another piece of toast atop the foie gras. Drizzle the plate with the Port Wine Glaze (recipe follows) and serve immediately.

Yield: 8 servings

BRIOCHE

4 tablespoons active dry yeast
¼ cup sugar
1½ teaspoons salt
⅓ cup warm water (105°–110°)
3½ cups all-purpose flour

5 eggs, room temperature
1 pound unsalted butter, cut into tablespoons, room temperature

In a large mixing bowl, mix the yeast, sugar, and salt with the warm water. Let stand for 15 minutes. Add the flour and mix on low speed with an electric mixer. Slowly add the eggs, 1 at a time, mixing well and scraping down the sides of the bowl. Add the butter, 1 tablespoon at a time. Continue beating for 5 minutes. Cover with plastic wrap and let rise until doubled in size, about 1½ hours.

Punch down the dough, re-cover with plastic wrap, and refrigerate overnight.

Place the dough into a large loaf pan and let rise again until it is ¾ of the way up the side of the pan, about 1½ hours.

Preheat the oven to 375°.

Bake loaves for 45 minutes. Remove from heat and let cool before slicing.

FIG RELISH

1 tablespoon butter
2 tablespoons minced shallots
1½ cups whole fig preserves, small dice
2 tablespoons brown sugar
2 tablespoons sherry vinegar
2 tablespoons minced celery
2 tablespoons small diced red peppers
½ teaspoon fresh thyme leaves, chopped
salt and pepper to taste

Melt the butter over low heat in a small saucepan. Cook the shallots 3 minutes. Add the diced figs and brown sugar and cook 5–6 minutes, stirring often to prevent sticking and burning. Add the sherry vinegar, celery, and red bell peppers and lower the heat. Cook 10 minutes, stirring often. Add the thyme, salt, and black pepper and remove from heat. When ready to use, warm relish slowly in a small sauté pan over a low heat.

Yield: 1½ cups

PORT WINE GLAZE

1 cup chicken stock
1 tablespoon brown sugar
1 cup port wine
2 teaspoons balsamic vinegar

Place all ingredients in a small saucepan. Simmer and reduce until mixture forms a thick syrup.

Yield: ¼ cup

Frisee and Warm Mushroom Salad

One of my favorite New York restaurants is Gotham Bar and Grill. Alfred Portale created a beautiful frisee salad that is served for lunch in that great space on East 12ᵗʰ Street. This is my take on that excellent recipe.

18 large shiitake mushroom caps, stems removed
1 cup olive oil, divided
1 teaspoon kosher salt, divided
½ teaspoon black pepper, freshly ground, divided
½ pound slab bacon, cut into ½-inch cubes
1 tablespoon Dijon mustard
¼ cup sherry vinegar
8 cups frisee lettuce, cleaned and dried completely
1 tablespoon shallot, minced
½ teaspoon garlic, minced
½ teaspoon fresh thyme, chopped
6 ounces feta cheese, crumbled

Place the shiitake mushrooms in a mixing bowl and toss with ¼ cup of the olive oil, half of the salt, and half of the pepper. Lay them out in a single layer on a baking sheet. Roast the mushrooms at 375° for 6–8 minutes. Remove from the oven, and allow to cool until cool enough to be handled. Cut the mushrooms into thick slices and place in a large mixing bowl. Hold mushrooms in a warm place while you prepare the remaining ingredients.

Place 1 tablespoon of the olive oil in a medium sauté pan over low-medium heat. Place the cubed bacon in the heated oil and cook until bacon becomes brown and crispy. Stir the bacon often to make sure all sides become brown. Remove bacon from the grease using a slotted spoon and place on paper towel to drain. Save 3 tablespoons of the bacon fat and keep it warm.

In a small mixing bowl, whisk together the mustard, remaining salt and pepper, and vinegar. Whisking constantly, drizzle in the remaining olive oil and the reserved bacon grease.

Toss the warm mushrooms with three quarters of the dressing. Add the frisee and half of the bacon and toss so that the frisee is well coated. Divide the salad onto 6–8 serving dishes. Toss the shallot, garlic, thyme, and crumbled feta cheese with the remaining quarter of the dressing. Sprinkle feta cheese and the remaining bacon over the tops of each salad and serve immediately.

Yield: 6–8 servings

Lobster and Brie Bisque

This bisque was created for a Purple Parrot Café New Year's Eve menu in the early 1990s. It reappears almost every time we have a special event in the restaurant.

2 1½-pound lobsters, cooked and cleaned (reserve meat for soup and shells for stock)
½ gallon lobster stock*
1 cup white wine
1 cup tomato paste
2 cups whipping cream
1 pound brie, rind removed and cubed
¼ cup butter
⅓ cup flour
½ cup sour cream
1 bay leaf
½ teaspoon dried thyme or 2 teaspoons fresh chopped thyme
2–3 tablespoons fresh chives, chopped

In a large saucepan, bring the lobster stock, white wine, and tomato paste to a boil. Continue to cook, allowing stock to reduce by half.

Meanwhile, in a double boiler, heat the whipping cream and cheese together until the cheese has melted.

In a medium skillet, heat the butter and add flour to make a blond roux. Add cream, bay leaf, and cheese mixture to the reduced stock. Add roux and bring to a boil. Add thyme. Lower heat and add reserved lobster meat.

Place sour cream in a squirt bottle. Ladle soup into serving bowls and decorate the top with thin ribbons of sour cream and freshly chopped chives.

*To make lobster stock, follow the same procedure and recipe for Shrimp Stock (p. 35). It is important to clean the lobster bodies well to remove organs and gills prior to making the stock.

Yield: 3 quarts

Lamb Chops
with Mint Compound Butter

Lamb and mint are a perfect pairing and one I think is more special than beef when served at a formal dinner. The rosettes are pretty, but if you don't have a pastry bag, roll the softened butter in parchment paper and freeze. When completely frozen, slice 1/2-inch discs and top lamb with cold butter.

MINT COMPOUND BUTTER

1 teaspoon olive oil
2 teaspoons shallot, minced
½ teaspoon fresh garlic, minced
1 teaspoon kosher salt
2 tablespoons Riesling wine
½ teaspoon black pepper, freshly ground
1 tablespoon mint jelly
2 tablespoons fresh mint, chopped fine
¾ cup unsalted butter, softened
1 teaspoon Worcestershire sauce
½ teaspoon hot sauce

In a small sauté pan, heat the oil over low heat. Cook the shallot, garlic, and salt 3–4 minutes. Add the wine, black pepper, and mint jelly and cook for 5 minutes more, stirring often to prevent sticking and burning. Add fresh mint and cook for 1 minute. Remove from heat and cool completely.

Place the softened butter in a mixing bowl and, using a rubber spatula, blend together Worcestershire, hot sauce, and the cooled mint mixture.

Line a large platter or small baking sheet with wax paper.
Place the butter compound in a pastry bag with a medium star tip attached. Pipe rosettes, approximately 2–3 teaspoons in size, onto the waxed paper. You should have 16 rosettes when finished. Refrigerate or freeze until needed.

**Not with a Whimper,
But a Bang.**
At midnight the night sky flashes with a lightning storm of fireworks. Dogs bark all over the neighborhood, and the smell of sulfur drifts in small clouds. A year ended and another begun.

LAMB CHOPS

2 tablespoons olive oil
4 racks of lamb, cut into 16 double-bone chops
1 tablespoon kosher salt
1 teaspoon black pepper, freshly ground

Preheat oven to 375°.

In a large skillet, heat the olive oil over high heat. Season lamb chops with salt and pepper. Place lamb in the hot skillet and sear each side until golden brown, 3–4 minutes on each side. Place the seared lamb on a baking sheet and continue cooking in the oven 6–7 minutes. Use a meat thermometer to check internal temperature, 125° for medium-rare.

Once cooked, remove the lamb and place 2 chops on each serving plate. Top each lamb chop with a rosette of the butter and serve immediately.

Yield: 8 servings

Au Gratin Potatoes

These are great when paired with an elegant entrée for a formal dinner, but they're also a perfect accompaniment for a midweek steak-and-potatoes dinner. Make sure to have all of your ingredients ready before you slice the potatoes. The dish must be made quickly to keep the potatoes from oxidizing. DO NOT place sliced potatoes in ice water, as they will lose their starch and thickening ability.

¼ cup unsalted butter, softened, divided
1¼ cups heavy whipping cream
½ teaspoon Creole Seasoning (recipe page 21)
2 pounds Idaho potatoes, peeled and cut into ¼-inch slices
1 teaspoon salt
½ teaspoon black pepper
½ cup Gruyère cheese, grated
¾ cup Parmesan cheese, freshly grated

Preheat oven to 350°. Butter a 2-quart baking dish with 1–2 tablespoons of the softened butter.

Combine the whipping cream and Creole Seasoning.

Arrange a layer of potatoes in the baking dish and sprinkle a small amount of the salt, pepper, cheeses, and cream over the potatoes. Continue this process until all of the potatoes are layered in the baking dish with the cheese, salt, pepper, and cream.

Dot the top of the potatoes with the remaining softened butter. Cover with foil and bake for 25 minutes. Remove the foil and continue baking for 45 minutes, until the potatoes are tender. Let stand 5 minutes before serving.

Yield: 8 servings

Chocolate Croissant
Bread Pudding

Linda Nance created this dessert several years ago for a Mother's Day brunch. It is my wife's favorite dessert at the restaurant.

12 ounces chocolate chips, divided
1 teaspoon vanilla extract
1¼ cups cream
½ cup milk
½ cup sugar, divided
2 eggs
6 egg yolks
⅛ teaspoon salt
6 croissants

Lightly butter an 8¼ x 8½ x 2½-inch ceramic baking dish.

Melt half of the chocolate chips in a double boiler. Heat the vanilla, cream, and milk with half the sugar and pour over melted chocolate. Combine the other half of the sugar with the eggs and yolks and whip until light and fluffy. Add salt. Temper the hot chocolate mixture slowly into the egg mixture.

Cut the croissants in half. Submerge the bottom halves of the croissants into the custard mixture and soak 10 minutes. Gently remove them from the custard and cover the bottom of the baking dish with the soaked croissant halves. Sprinkle the remaining chocolate chips over the soaked croissants.

Soak the tops of the croissants in the remaining custard mixture for 10 minutes. Gently remove them from the custard and arrange them atop the chocolate chips. Pour any remaining custard over the croissants. Cover and refrigerate overnight.

Preheat oven to 325°.

Remove the prepared bread pudding from the refrigerator 1 hour before baking. Press the croissants down to make sure all of the custard has been absorbed into the croissants. Cover the bread pudding with a sheet of wax paper, followed by a sheet of aluminum foil. Place the covered baking dish in a large roasting pan and fill the pan with hot water so that it comes 1½ inches up the sides of the baking dish. Bake 25 minutes.

Remove the foil-and-wax-paper cover and bake for 20–30 minutes more. The bread pudding should jiggle slightly but have no liquid custard remaining. Remove from the oven and allow the bread pudding to rest for 30 minutes before serving.

Place a small pool of the Bourbon Crème Anglaise (recipe follows) on each serving dish. Cut the bread pudding into 6–8 portions and place each piece in the center of the crème anglais, serve immediately.

Yield: 6–8 servings

Bourbon Crème Anglaise

1 cup cream
½ cup half-and-half
¼ cup bourbon
1 teaspoon vanilla extract
¾ cup sugar, divided
4 egg yolks

In a stainless steel pot bring the cream, half-and-half, bourbon, vanilla, and half of the sugar to a simmer. While the mixture is heating, combine the yolks and remaining sugar in a mixing bowl and whip until light in color.

Slowly add the hot cream mixture to the yolks while stirring constantly. Return the mixture to the pot and cook over a low-medium flame, stirring constantly. Cook until the mixture becomes thick enough to coat a spoon or spatula. Remove from the heat and cool down in an ice bath.

Yield: 8 servings

Funeral Fare

Baked Potato Soup

Potato Salad

The Last Pimiento Cheese Ever

Corn Pudding

Chicken Jambalaya

Whole Marinated and Smoked Beef Tenderloin

Shrimp, Crab, and Andouille Gumbo

Six Classic Finger Sandwiches

Banana Pudding with No-Fail Meringue

The Crossing
The first date I had with my wife was to see *Our Town* by Thornton Wilder. The cemetery scene suggests a perspective on life that made everything make sense. Or, maybe I was just in love.

Baked Potato Soup

Rich, hearty, and a crowd-pleaser. Freezes well, but you'll have a hard time not eating it all immediately.

½ pound bacon, diced
1 tablespoon butter
1 cup onion, small dice
½ cup celery, small dice
½ cup carrot, small dice
2 teaspoons garlic, minced
2 teaspoons salt
1 teaspoon black pepper, freshly ground
2 pounds potatoes, peeled and cut into ½-inch cubes
1½ quarts chicken broth
½ cup butter
¾ cup flour
2 cups heavy whipping cream
1½ cups milk
1 cup sour cream
1 cup Monterey jack cheese, shredded
1 teaspoon hot sauce
½ cup green onion, freshly chopped

Place bacon and butter in a 6-quart stockpot over medium heat and cook bacon until golden brown. Drain excess bacon grease and add vegetables, garlic, salt, and pepper. Cook 4–5 minutes. Add potatoes and chicken broth and bring to a slow simmer. Cook until potatoes are tender, approximately 15 minutes.

In a separate skillet, melt butter and stir in flour to make a roux. Cook until the roux is light blond and gently whisk roux into soup mixture. Be careful not to break up the potatoes. Add remaining ingredients and bring to a simmer once more. Remove from heat and serve.

Yield: 1 gallon

Potato Salad

Potato salad is one of the quintessential funeral foods. This is the basic mustard variety with a slight twist.

6 cups Idaho potatoes, peeled and cut into a large dice
3 quarts water
4 teaspoons salt, divided
2 cups mayonnaise
½ cup yellow mustard
1 tablespoon Dijon mustard
2 tablespoons cider vinegar
1 teaspoon white pepper
1½ teaspoons black pepper, freshly ground
1 cup green onion, chopped
1 cup red bell pepper, small dice
1 cup celery, small dice
4 eggs, hard-boiled and chopped
¼ cup sweet pickle relish

Place potatoes and 2 teaspoons of salt in water and simmer on low heat until potatoes are tender. Drain and allow to cool.

Combine mayonnaise, yellow mustard, Dijon, vinegar, white pepper, black pepper, and remaining 2 teaspoons salt to form a dressing. Add potatoes and all other ingredients to the dressing and mix well.

Yield: 2 quarts

The Last Pimiento Cheese Ever

The flavors in this recipe are more complex than the standard pimiento-cheese-and-mayo versions. The bacon adds smokiness. Roasting bell peppers on your own is simple and worth the effort.

½ cup cooked bacon, chopped
½ pound extra-sharp white cheddar, roughly grated and at room temperature
½ pound extra-sharp yellow cheddar, roughly grated and at room temperature
1 cup roasted red bell peppers, chopped
¾ cup mayonnaise
½ cup green onions, chopped
2 teaspoons garlic, minced
2 teaspoons Creole Seasoning (recipe page 21)
Salt and freshly ground black pepper

In a large skillet, cook the bacon until brown and crisp, approximately 6–7 minutes. Transfer to paper towels to drain and cool. Using the paddle attachment of an electric mixer, gently combine all ingredients until well blended.

Cover and refrigerate for at least 2–3 hours to allow flavors to meld.

Bare Trees
When the leaves fall the stark architecture of the trees can be appreciated. When I was a child, this kind of tree inspired plans for building tree houses.

Corn Pudding

This recipe should be a supper staple throughout the year. Double the hot sauce and pepper if you're feeling adventurous.

3 cups Silver Queen corn (4–5 ears)
2 cups heavy cream
1 cup half-and-half
1½ tablespoons sugar
2 teaspoons salt
3 eggs + 3 yolks
1½ teaspoons black pepper, freshly ground
1 teaspoon hot sauce
2 teaspoons onion, minced

Preheat oven to 300°.

Combine all ingredients and mix well. Place in 2-quart baking dish. Place dish into a larger dish and place in oven. Pour hot water into the larger dish so water comes up halfway on the sides of the corn pudding dish. Bake 40 minutes. Remove from oven and allow pudding to cool 10–15 minutes before serving.

Yield: 10–12 servings

Chicken Jambalaya

Not the typical funeral fare, but a great one-dish for covered-dish suppers, progressive dinners, and all occasions.

2 pounds andouille sausage, or any mild smoked pork sausage, sliced about ¼-inch thick
3 pounds chicken thigh meat, boneless and skinless, cut into 1½-inch pieces
1 tablespoon Creole Seasoning (recipe page 21)
2 cups yellow onion, medium dice
1½ cups celery, medium dice
1½ cup green bell pepper, medium dice
2 tablespoons fresh garlic, minced
1 teaspoon dried thyme
3 bay leaves
1 pound long-grain rice
1 14-ounce can diced tomatoes
1 tablespoon Worcestershire sauce
1 tablespoon hot sauce
1 quart + 1 cup chicken broth, heated
1 tablespoon kosher salt

Place a large heavy-duty cast-iron skillet or dutch oven (2-gallon capacity) on high heat.

Place the sausage in the hot skillet and brown evenly, stirring often to prevent burning. When the sausage is browned, carefully remove the excess fat.

Season the chicken with the Creole Seasoning and add to skillet. Brown the chicken evenly and cook 20 minutes. Add onion, celery, and bell pepper and lower heat to medium. Cook for 10 minutes, stirring often.

Add in the garlic, thyme, and bay leaves and cook 5 minutes more. Stir in the rice and cook until the rice grains are hot. Add the canned tomatoes, Worcestershire sauce, hot sauce, chicken broth, and salt. Stir well to prevent the rice from clumping together.

Lower the heat until the Jambalaya is just barely simmering and cover. Cook 30 minutes.

Yield: 12–14 servings

Whole Marinated and Smoked Beef Tenderloin

This is the most unique and appreciated food item one can bring to a friend's home. You'll blow them away. Hardly anyone roasts an entire beef tenderloin and gives it away. After you try this recipe, you'll wonder why.

1 cup Wishbone Italian Dressing
¼ cup Worcestershire sauce
5-pound whole beef tenderloin, cleaned and trimmed
2 tablespoons Steak Seasoning (recipe follows)

Combine the Italian dressing and Worcestershire sauce. Coat the tenderloin with the marinade and wrap in plastic wrap. Refrigerate overnight.

Prepare the charcoal according to the directions on the grill for slow barbecuing.

Sprinkle the steak seasoning over the entire tenderloin and cook on the prepared grill for 1–2 hours, until an internal temperature of 125° is achieved. Allow the meat to rest 10 minutes before slicing and serving.

Yield: 10–14 servings

STEAK SEASONING

½ cup Lawry's Seasoned Salt
⅓ cup black pepper
¼ cup lemon pepper
2 tablespoons garlic salt
2 tablespoons granulated garlic
1 tablespoons onion powder

Combine all and mix well. Store in an airtight container.

Shrimp, Crab, and Andouille Gumbo

Give me gumbo, warm French bread, and a little time, and I'm a happy man—especially when I come back for seconds.

½ cup canola oil
¾ cup flour
2 tablespoons filé powder
1 cup onion, diced
½ cup celery, diced
½ cup bell pepper, diced
1½ cups andouille sausage, sliced
1 pound small shrimp
2 tablespoons garlic, minced
2 teaspoons salt
1½ teaspoons black pepper
2 teaspoons Creole Seasoning (recipe page 21)
1½ teaspoons dried basil
1 teaspoon dried thyme
2 quarts shrimp stock (recipe page 35)
1 cup tomatoes, diced (canned or fresh)
1 pound crab claw meat
1 tablespoon hot sauce
¼ teaspoon cayenne pepper
 cooked white rice as needed

In a large skillet, combine oil, flour, and filé powder to form a roux. Cook over medium heat, stirring often until roux is very dark (do not burn). Add vegetables, andouille, shrimp, garlic, salt, pepper, Creole Seasoning, basil, and thyme and continue to cook for 5–7 minutes, stirring constantly to prevent burning.

In a separate pot, bring shrimp stock and tomatoes to a boil. Slowly add roux mixture to boiling stock and mix well. Add crabmeat and lower heat to a slow simmer. Cook 10 minutes more. Add hot sauce and cayenne pepper.

Place ¼ cup of white rice in each serving bowl, then pour gumbo over rice and serve.
Yield: 1 gallon

Six Classic Finger Sandwiches

Make sure to cover the sandwiches with a damp paper towel and plastic wrap. Great for a party.

CHICKEN SALAD SANDWICHES

1 pound chicken breasts
1 teaspoon poultry seasoning
½ onion, quartered
1 celery stalk, cut into 2-inch pieces
1 bay leaf
1 quart water
2 hard-boiled eggs, chopped
1 teaspoons Creole Seasoning (recipe page 21)
½ teaspoon Lawry's Seasoned Salt
⅓ cup mayonnaise
1 tablespoon Creole mustard
1 can water chestnuts, roughly chopped
¼ cup toasted pecans
¼ cup celery, minced
2 tablespoons red onion, minced
1 teaspoon lemon juice
⅛ teaspoon ground black pepper
2–3 tablespoons chicken stock
10 slices white bread

Place the chicken along with the salt, pepper, onion, celery stalk, and bay leaf in a large stock pot. Cover with water and bring to a boil. Lower the heat and simmer until the chicken is cooked through. Remove chicken from pot, reserve the broth, and cool. Cut the chicken into a very small dice and place in a large bowl. Add the remaining ingredients and mix well.

Divide the chicken salad onto 5 slices of the bread and spread it evenly to the sides. Top each sandwich with the remaining slices of bread. Cut the crusts from the sandwiches and cut each sandwich into 3 rectangles. Cover well and refrigerate until needed.

Yield: 15 finger sandwiches

A Little Light Drizzle
Rain isn't always a downpour or a heavy mist. There is a silence I associate with this experience. It creates reflective moods as well as puddles.

PIMIENTO CHEESE SANDWICHES

1 recipe The Last Pimiento Cheese Ever (recipe page 220)
10 slices white bread

Divide the pimiento cheese onto 5 slices of the bread and spread it evenly to the sides. Top each sandwich with one of the remaining slices of bread. Cut the crusts from the sandwiches and cut each sandwich into 3 rectangles. Cover well and refrigerate until needed.

TOMATO, BACON, AND BASIL SANDWICHES

½ cup mayonnaise
2 tablespoons fresh basil, chopped
½ teaspoon black pepper, freshly ground
10 slices thick bacon, cooked and chopped
20 thin tomato slices
10 slices sourdough bread

Mix together the mayonnaise, basil, and ground pepper. Spread the mayonnaise mixture evenly over 5 slices of the bread. Sprinkle each slice of bread with the chopped bacon. Arrange 4 slices of tomato on each piece of bread, making sure to cover the entire surface of the bread. Top with the remaining slices of the bread. Cut the crusts from the sandwiches and cut each sandwich into 3 rectangles. Cover well and refrigerate until needed.

HOMEMADE BOURSIN CHEESE AND CUCUMBER SANDWICHES

To make the cheese:
8 ounces cream cheese, softened
1 tablespoon salted butter, softened
½ teaspoon Creole Seasoning (recipe page 21)
¼ teaspoon garlic, minced
⅛ teaspoon each, thyme, oregano, rosemary, chives, basil, dill, sage
1 teaspoon fresh parsley, chopped fine
2 tablespoon half-and-half
1 teaspoon sherry vinegar
¼ teaspoon Worcestershire sauce
⅓ cup sour cream

Place all ingredients in the bowl of an electric mixer. Using the paddle attachment, beat on high speed until all ingredients are well incorporated, scraping sides of the bowl occasionally to ensure all ingredients are combined.

To make sandwiches:
1 cucumber, peeled and sliced into very thin rounds
½ cup red onion, shaved
12 pieces wheat bread

Spread the Boursin Cheese mixture evenly over 6 slices of the bread. Arrange the cucumber slices on each piece of bread, making sure to cover the entire surface of the bread. Divide the red onions evenly atop the cucumber slices and top with the remaining slices of the bread. Cut the crusts from the sandwiches and cut each sandwich into 3 rectangles. Cover well and refrigerate until needed.

EGG SALAD SANDWICHES

9 hard-boiled eggs, peeled and chopped
⅓ cup mayonnaise
1 tablespoon sweet pickle relish
1½ teaspoons whole grain mustard
1 tablespoon fresh chives, chopped
2 teaspoons fresh parsley, chopped
¾ teaspoon kosher salt
¼ teaspoon black pepper, freshly ground
10 slices wheat bread

Combine all ingredients except bread and mix well. Refrigerate until ready to make the sandwiches.

Divide the egg salad onto 5 slices of the bread and spread it evenly to the sides. Top each sandwich with one of the remaining slices of bread. Cut the crusts from the sandwiches and cut each sandwich into 3 rectangles. Cover well and refrigerate until needed.

SMOKED SALMON AND WATERCRESS SANDWICHES

8 ounces cream cheese, softened
2 tablespoons capers, rinsed and chopped
1 tablespoon shallot, minced
1 tablespoon fresh dill, chopped
2 teaspoons lemon juice
6 ounces smoked salmon, chopped fine
1 bunch watercress, rinsed and dried very well
10 slices rye bread

Using an electric mixer, whip the cream cheese until it is light and fluffy. Add the capers, shallot, dill, and lemon juice and mix well. Using a rubber spatula, fold in the smoked salmon pieces. Divide the cream cheese mixture onto 5 slices of the bread and spread it evenly to the sides. Remove any large stems from the watercress and top the cream mixture with a thin layer of watercress. Top each sandwich with one of the remaining slices of bread. Cut the crusts from the sandwiches and cut each sandwich into 3 rectangles. Cover well and refrigerate until needed.

Banana Pudding
with No-Fail Meringue

Make sure to prepare the custard before slicing the bananas so they don't oxidize. This is great when eaten warm straight out of the oven, or cold out of the refrigerator. I like to use more bananas than what the recipe calls for, others might want more cookies and less bananas. Fee free to improvise.

1 cup sugar
6 tablespoons flour
pinch of salt
4 egg yolks (reserve whites for meringue)
2 cups milk
2 teaspoons vanilla extract
6 tablespoons butter
4 ripe bananas, peeled and sliced
vanilla wafers

Preheat oven to 350°.

Combine sugar, flour, salt, egg yolks, milk, and vanilla in a small non-reactive saucepan. Cook over low heat, stirring constantly until the pudding thickens. Remove from heat and slowly add butter until incorporated.

Butter a 2-quart baking dish. Arrange the vanilla wafers around the outside and across the bottom of the baking dish. Spread a layer of custard over the wafers. Place sliced bananas on top of custard and spoon the remaining custard over bananas, spreading evenly.

NO-FAIL MERINGUE

4 egg whites
½ cup sugar
½ teaspoon cream of tartar
2 tablespoons cornstarch
½ cup water

Combine water and cornstarch in a small sauce pot and cook slowly until mixture becomes gelatinous. Allow mixture to cool.

In a large mixing bowl begin beating whites until they begin to get foamy and increase in volume. Slowly add in the sugar and cream of tartar and continue to whip until soft peaks form. Add in the gel and whip until medium hard peaks form. Spread over banana pudding and bake 8-10 minutes at 350°.

Yield: 8–10 servings

Rump Roast
Growing up across from a pasture, I learned a lot about the cycle of life. All things come to an end.

Index